MW01119528

THE WAY HE LOVED ME

By
Heather Tanti

First Edition
First printing: 2017
ISBN: 978-1981914050
Published by: Heather Tanti
Edited by: Geesey Editorial Services
Illustrations by: Safa Shaqsy

CONTENTS

CHAPTER ONE

"You should ask him out," Trish prompted, jabbing me in the side with her elbow. I rolled my eyes at her. It wasn't uncommon for my best friend of nine years to play match-maker, refusing to give up until I had finally landed a boyfriend.

"I don't have time to date." It was my standard reply. Trish sighed loudly and pretended to bang her head against her locker. I laughed and grabbed my English textbook, shoving it into my backpack.

"I'll see you after class!" I hugged her quickly and hurried down the hall.

School had always been my main focus. My parents were strict, and as an only child the pressure to be the very best was strong. I was in my senior year of high school and had never even had a boyfriend. It wasn't until Trish had told me about losing her virginity and how I was missing out on the best years of my life, that I had really thought my lack of dating experience to have been a problem. 'It was amazing,' Trish had gushed, describing in way too much detail how her first time had gone. I had always told myself that it would happen when it was meant to, and despite the pressures around me, I still felt strongly about that.

The warning bell sounded just as I took my seat at the front of the class. I know, teacher's pet much? It didn't bother me that I had gained the reputation of the good girl; what bothered me were the not-so-quiet whispers about how "square" I was, and how I had probably never even seen a guy naked before. Was this really all the girls cared about at our age?

Mr. Tilson walked in, groggily giving his "Good morning, class" announcement while holding a mug of steaming black coffee. The teacher began to write the date on the board as the classroom door opened, and *he* walked in. By he, I mean the boy Trish said I should ask out, the boy who stood there confidently, giving me a smile that held so much mystery. No, this wasn't just any boy; he would be my undoing, my wrecking ball and the means to my end. Unfortunately, I was never to know just how bad he would be for me until it was too late, so when he walked into the room and gave me that smile, I shyly smiled back, looked away, and opened up my textbook.

His name was Jason, and he sat directly behind me. The classroom held about four empty seats, most near the back, yet here he was at the front of the class, so close I imagined I could feel his breath on the back of my neck. I tried to pretend I didn't notice … until a finger tapped me on the shoulder. I turned around and my green eyes met the deep blue of his.

"Can I borrow a pen?" It was such a simple question, yet it opened the door to so much more. I stared at him a moment too long before hastily digging through my pencil case and handing him a blue pen.

"Thanks," he said, giving me a quick wink that made my stomach summersault. *What the heck is wrong with me? Get a grip, Amy!* I told myself as I turned around and tried to focus on the teacher's voice.

The end of the day bell sounded and I bolted from my seat, rushing down the hall to my locker. I could see Trish coming; she was flirting with the captain of the basketball team. She smiled when she saw me, raising her eyebrows as if to say, *Do you see this hottie?* I giggled and put my books in my locker, closed it, and waited for Trish to do the same.

We left the school, pulling our sweaters tighter against the damp April weather. I gave her a hug bye as she climbed onto the bus and I made my way down the street towards home. I heard his footsteps before he even reached my side.

"You're one fast chick," he said, pretending to breathe heavily. "You left class so fast that I didn't get a chance to give you my number." We had stopped walking now, and I looked at him, amused.

"What makes you think that I wanted your number?" I put my hand on my hip for dramatic effect.

"Because you do," he said, holding his hand out for my cell phone. I raised my eyebrows in disbelief.

"You're serious, aren't you?" I laughed.

He kept his arm outstretched, his eyes on mine. "I never joke about giving a pretty girl my number."

I blushed and fumbled in my purse for my cell phone. He took it and quickly typed in his number, raised it up and snapped a picture of a goofy face before handing it back to me.

"There," he said, "now there's no reason for you to disappear on me." Once again, he gave me that mysterious smile before turning around and walking in the other direction.

Later that night, I sat on my bed staring at his picture and the seven numbers that would bring two worlds together. I bit my lip as my fingers hovered over the keys.

Amy: Hey…

Jason: Hey, beautiful.

That was it. There was no going back. No delete button, and no backspace to erase the choice I had made that very moment. I was hooked with two simple words, and this is where my story would begin.

CHAPTER TWO

I was never good at sleeping in. Saturday mornings still had me awake at sunrise, despite being a teenager. I stretched and rolled onto my side, reaching for my cell phone. I clicked the home screen. 6:05 a.m. Yep, I was crazy. I clicked on Jason's name, opening up our message history.

'Hey, beautiful' sat blissfully on my screen, making me smile like an idiot. I chewed my bottom lip, a nervous habit of mine, and began to type.

Amy: Good morning, what are you up to today?

Slowly I got out of bed, not expecting a reply at this time of the morning. As I was brushing my teeth, the familiar ding of a text message went off. I put my toothbrush down and picked up my phone.

Jason: Morning, early bird! Did you

forget we had a date today?

I searched my brain for a recollection of any plans made. There was no way I'd forget a date with Jason.

Amy: A date??!! I don't remember this plan!
Jason: Be ready at 8:10 AM. Dress warm.

That was all he said. No hints, no asking if I wanted to go out, just a message to be ready. I stood there looking in the mirror at myself and smiled. I was about to go on my first date! I rummaged through my drawers, pulling out my favorite dark blue jeans and pink sweatshirt that fit my slender frame well. I brushed my long brown hair until it was smooth and shiny and applied some mascara to make the green in my eyes stand out. Once satisfied with my appearance, I checked my phone. 7:45 a.m. Still lots of time to spare.

I sat on my doorstep and listened as the birds chirped and the odd car drove by. I watched carefully for any sign of Jason before realizing I had no idea what kind of car he drove, or if he even drove at all. I also realized I hadn't given him my address and opened my phone to send it to him. As I started typing, tires came screeching around the corner and a red Sunfire pulled to a harsh stop in front of my house. I stopped typing and looked up to see Jason sitting in his car, grinning at me. All thoughts of how he knew where I lived left my mind as I got into his car. That was my first mistake.

Metal music blasted loudly as I climbed into the car, he politely turned it down and put on a country station before turning it back up and putting the car into drive. He didn't say anything as I buckled my seatbelt, but he was smiling as he turned down a back road with one hand on the steering wheel and one confidently placed on my knee. I squirmed nervously at his touch. He looked over at me and winked, once again sending me into a puddle of mush. I couldn't believe what was happening, and willed myself to stop freaking out like a little school girl. This was new, yes, and a little frightening, but in a good way. Plus Jason was hot, and isn't that what matters when it comes to high school dating?

"Where are we going?" I asked, as the back roads went from empty fields to thick forests. My stomach was tight with anticipation.

"You'll see," is all he said, as he turned up the music to a slow country song. I looked out the window, still fully aware of the warmth of his hand on my knee; it hadn't moved except to give a light squeeze here and there. We turned down a dirt road, its path winding into the forest. We drove for about five more minutes before the trees opened up to a little clearing of grass with an old swing set. He put the car in park, opened his door, and looked over at me.

"Don't move," he said as he opened the trunk and grabbed something before opening my door and helping me out. He was holding a blanket and a cooler. I smiled and looked up at him.

"Are we having a picnic?"

He smiled in return and placed his hand on the small of my back. My muscles tensed at first, then relaxed against his touch as I let him lead me towards the grass.

Jason spread the blanket out on the damp grass, opened up the cooler and pulled out cheese and crackers, and a bottle of champagne. He sat down and patted the blanket beside him. I paused nervously before sitting down.

"Isn't it a little early for champagne?" Truth be told I had never had a drink in my life. He pulled out two wine glasses, popped the cork on the bottle, and poured them full of sparkling golden liquid.

"Aren't you too old for such silly rules?" he replied, clinking his glass with mine. I put the glass to my lips and took a small sip, the bubbles danced on my tongue before warming my insides.

"Have you always been such a romantic?" I was finishing my second glass of wine, feeling braver than I ever have, thanks to some liquid courage. He was leaning back on his elbows, his long sleeve shirt tight against the muscles in his arms. I couldn't help but stare and he knew it.

"Only with the right girl would I put such effort," he said, tucking my hair behind my ear. I looked down, a blush creeping into my cheeks. His fingers lifted my chin until we were face to face.

"Never hide your smile from me, it's beautiful. Understand?"

My eyes were wide and drinking in every bit of him in the fairytale date he had created. I nodded in agreement.

"Good girl," he said softly.

CHAPTER THREE

The next week was a blur. I must have spent nearly every spare second with Jason. We would find each other in the halls between classes, sneak texts during class, and he would drive me home after school (dropping me off down the road so my parents didn't freak). He was the perfect gentleman so much so that we hadn't even kissed yet. Trish nagged me constantly about that.

"When are you going to kiss? How have you not done it yet? You're killing me!" I laughed most times, brushing it off as Trish being Trish, but a small part of me worried that if I didn't initiate some sort of move, he would lose interest in me. He never pressured nor asked for anything from me, but was that simply because he was just being nice? Surely he has some expectations; after all, he's a guy.

School dragged on that day as my mind replayed Trish's words. I had to make a move. I didn't want to lose Jason. I climbed into his car and closed the door. Buckling my seatbelt, I looked over at him and smiled.

"Hey, beautiful. Missed you today," he said as he drove down the road. We were approaching the street by my house. His hand rested firmly on my knee. I put my hand over his and squeezed it.

"Stop the car here," I said quietly.

He did so with a look of confusion.

"Everything okay, babe?"

"You like me, right?" I asked, already regretting the words as I said them. He gave me his smile and squeezed my knee.

"Of course I do! Why are you asking?" He looked genuinely concerned, which made me decide to just be honest with him.

"Trish thinks it's strange that we've never … you know … kissed yet." My eyes were focused on my lap as I picked at a thread in my jeans.

"Why is that strange?" His voice was more serious this time, and I braved a glance at him. He was completely focused on me.

"She says you will lose interest if I don't initiate some sort of move." My cheeks were burning.

He laughed and lifted my chin to face him. "Are you happy?"

"Yes, of course," I replied.

"Do you want to kiss me?" he asked.
I bit my lower lip nervously before answering.

"Yes." It was barely a whisper, but it was enough for him to unbuckle his seatbelt, click open mine, and place his hand on the back of my neck. His touch on my skin was warm and comforting. My heart hammered in my chest as he looked at me.

"Close your eyes." I did as he said, while silently freaking out. I could feel his other hand leave my knee and cup the side of my face, his thumb brushing against my lower lip. Slowly he moved in and his lips pressed against mine, gentle and warm. My own body responded by parting my lips, inviting him in. His tongue grazed against mine. I could taste the cherry Coke on his breath. He pulled away and I opened my eyes, my chest rising and falling with anticipation.

"Did you like that?"

"Yes …"

His mouth found mine again and this time the kiss was deeper, more passionate. His hand on my neck pulled me further into the kiss until I was breathless and pulling away.

"Wow," was all I managed to say. Awesome, right? My first kiss ever and all I could say was *wow*.

Jason winked at me and put the car into drive, continuing towards my house. His hand went back to my knee, only this time it slid up a little higher and rested comfortably on my thigh. My pulse was through the roof by the time he reached my street.

"Text me later, babe," he said as I climbed out of the car.

"Thanks for the pep-talk," I replied as I smiled and waved goodbye. He drove off down the street, his wheels squealing with his increasing speed.

I pulled my phone out as I walked and opened up Trish's message.

> *Amy: Guess what!?*
> *Trish: WHAT!!??*
> *Amy: WE KISSED!!!*
> *Trish: Finally! How was it??*
> *Amy: OMG. Amazing! You were right, I was missing out! LOL*
> *Trish: Told ya! I want the juicy details tomorrow!*
> *Amy: Deal!* ☺

CHAPTER FOUR

I couldn't get enough of him. He was all I thought about from sunup to sundown. Jason had become my life after only two months of dating. Most would say it wasn't healthy to be so caught up in someone, but I had never felt happier. My parents noticed my incessant texting and frequent outings, so I decided it was time to tell them about Jason, and hopefully have their blessing to continue dating him.

My mom understood, and was almost thrilled, I think, probably because she was worried I'd never do anything but study in my room and never experience life. Dad was apprehensive, but, with a few rules, they both agreed to let me keep seeing him. Curfew was ten at night, no later, and I wasn't to let him get in the way of my studies. I nodded away eagerly, and hugged my parents, thanking them. Mom laughed at me and told me to get out before they changed their minds.

I immediately texted Jason.

Amy: Guess what???
Jason: What's up?!
Amy: I told my parents about us, and they didn't freak! No more sneaking around! ☺
Jason: That's wicked. Can I come by tonite?
Amy: Sure! I'll msg you after dinner. XOXO
Jason: see U soon XO

I asked my parents if Jason could come by after dinner and they agreed as long as they were introduced and my bedroom door stayed open. I rolled my eyes and kissed my mom on the cheek before carrying my plate to the sink. Once the dishes were done I texted Jason.

Amy: you can come over now ☺
Jason: Be there soon.

He showed up in blue jeans, a t-shirt, and a ball cap. He was everything amazing all wrapped up into the guy I was lucky enough to call mine. I smiled at him and gave him a quick kiss on the cheek before inviting him in. He removed his hat when he walked in and shook hands with my parents, already impressing my dad.

"It's nice to meet you, Jason. We've heard so much about you," my mom said, making me go red. Dad just nodded and smiled stiffly. After a few awkward moments I broke the silence.

"We're going to study in my room." I grabbed his hand and pulled him behind me.

"Door stays open," Mom yelled up the stairs. Jason chuckled and squeezed my hand as I pulled us into my room.

"Study, eh?" he said, his voice low and husky as he wrapped his arms around my waist. "I know what I'd like to study." His lips were trailing kisses down my neck. I glanced nervously over his shoulder to see if my parents were spying before I kissed him on the lips softly, then harder. It was easy to get lost in his kisses, it happened often. I moaned into his mouth as his hands roamed under my shirt. I pulled away quickly, breathless.

"Whoa, my parents are right outside!" I whispered. He pulled me back against him and smiled.

"That's what makes it more fun. Don't be a tease," he whispered in my ear.

Goosebumps prickled my skin, and a

feeling of unease came over me for the first time.

"No, Jason, stop. I don't want to get in trouble the first time they meet you!" I pulled his hands from my waist and took a step back. He looked at me, and an expression I hadn't seen before flashed across his face: anger.

"I'm just going to leave," he said.

"Wait, Jason–" He walked out of the room before I had a chance to speak. I stood there feeling confused and worried. Why had he been upset? I must have hurt his feelings or something.

An hour passed and I pulled out my phone. No messages were received since he left.

Amy: Hey…

Ten minutes passed and no response. Panic set in. I didn't want to ruin things between us for being a goody good.

Amy: I'm sorry. I didn't mean to upset you. Please forgive me?
Jason: It's okay, I forgive you. Just don't do that again, okay?
Amy: I promise, I don't want to lose you. I'm so happy with you."
Jason: You are my one and only. Don't forget it. XO
Amy: Goodnight, sweet dreams ☺
Jason: Night.

CHAPTER FIVE

The next day at school it was as if nothing had ever happened. He wrapped his arm around me in the hall and walked me to my first class. We stood outside the door and kissed slowly. He pulled away and smiled at me. Everything felt right again.

"See you in English, babe," he said as he headed off to class. I took my seat and said hi to Trish who gushed about how adorable Jason and I were. I felt like I was on cloud nine, and equally silly about getting worked up over last night. I was lucky to be with a guy like Jason, any girl would kill to have him as her boyfriend.

"Want to hang out tonight?" Trish asked as we walked to our last class.

"Yeah, that would be great!" It had been a while since we'd had any girl time. Turning the corner, I bumped into Zach, causing his books to scatter onto the floor.

"Oh, Zach, I'm so sorry! Let me help you pick them up." Zach was the sweet, nerdy boy I'd known all my life, the kid my parents had hoped would be my future husband. We used to be good friends until life and differences got in the way.

"Thanks, Amy, and don't sweat it. I was born with two left feet," he joked. I laughed and said bye, touching him on the shoulder to apologize once more. When I looked down the hall I saw Jason leaning against the wall by our English class. His face was stern. He looked upset. Oh no! Had he seen me with Zach? Did he think there was something between us? My heart raced as Trish and I made our way towards the classroom.

"You ok? You seem on edge now," Trish asked with concern. I faked a smile for her and told her I was fine, just nervous about the English test today.

"Since when do you get nervous about tests? You're Miss A plus." I laughed half-heartedly as we took our seats. I looked behind me at Jason, but he didn't look up. He was texting on his phone. I turned back and faced the blackboard, dread and panic erasing the earlier happiness I had felt.

I finished the test with plenty of time to spare and raised my hand to use the washroom. With hall pass in hand I headed out. The girls' bathroom was empty. I looked in the mirror and tried to understand what was happening, but the sound of the door opening interrupted my thoughts. Jason was standing there holding a hall pass.

"Um ... I think you have the wrong bathroom." I tried to sound light and funny, but it came out quiet and timid. Rather than laughing with me he locked the door behind him. My stomach tightened. What was he doing?

"Jason ... what are you doing? You can't be in here." I was subconsciously walking backwards away from him. My back pressed against the wall as he walked towards me.

"Do you think it's nice to flirt with other guys in front of me, Amy?" His voice sounded funny. It was different. Cold and calculated.

"I ... I wasn't flirting. That's Zach. He's a friend. I bumped into him and–"

The jolt of pain as his fist hit my ribs was like fire. I dropped to my knees, a silent cry on my lips. I didn't understand what was happening or why he had hurt me. His face was pure anger and hatred before quickly turning into one of sorrow and guilt.

"Oh, babe, I'm so sorry. I didn't mean to hurt you." He was on his knees beside me, wiping my tears.

Carefully, he lifted me to my feet and took my face in his hands. His eyes were the eyes I recognized again, all dark blue and charismatic. He pulled me against his chest and smoothed my hair over and over, repeating how sorry he was until finally I believed it. He kissed my lips and smiled. I smiled back weakly. We walked back to the classroom hand in hand as if everything was perfectly normal. As if my boyfriend hadn't just punched me in the girls' bathroom. As if my ribs didn't ache with every move I made. As if I was completely and perfectly okay. I took my seat once more as my phone buzzed in my pocket. I pulled it out and opened the message.

Jason: You're beautiful.

This was the moment I chose to make excuses for what had just happened. The moment I became that girl who hid behind a fake smile with the constant worry of doing something wrong. This was the moment I forgave Jason for hurting me and vowed to never speak to another boy again.

This was the moment that I let him own me.

CHAPTER SIX

It felt like forever since I was at Trish's house. I was exhausted and my ribs ached so bad it took all I had not to cry. We spent three hours looking at magazines, gossiping about who was dating who and finished with how lucky I was to have Jason. My stomach turned at his name; the truth about earlier threatening to bubble to the surface. Instead, I smiled and told Trish how happy I was and thankful to be with him. The evening hours crept in and I excused myself to head home to dinner, hugging Trish tighter than usual.

It was seven thirty by the time I finished dinner and headed to my room. I changed out of my clothes and stood in front of the mirror, my hands covering my mouth in shock. The right sides of my ribs were purple and blue, redness circling the borders of the bruise. I touched it gently and winced. *He didn't mean it,* I reminded myself. *It was an accident.* He apologized and I accepted. It was time to forget about the whole thing. My hands trembled as I pulled a loose t-shirt on and my pajama shorts and crawled into bed, making sure to lie on my left side. I placed my cell phone on the night table and closed my eyes, hoping to forget this nightmare. The buzz of a text message made sure I would never forget.

> *Jason: Hey, baby. I want to apologize again for today. I never want to hurt you. You are the best thing in my life. I will pick you up in the morning for school. Can't wait to see you! XOXO*

I put the phone back down and closed my eyes. In the darkness of sleep I willed myself to erase the memories of today and be more cautious with my actions around Jason. By the time my alarm went off at 6:30 a.m., I felt a lot better. The only memory remaining was the ache in my ribs, and even that I chose to ignore.

He knocked on my door at precisely 7:45 a.m. My mom answered as I came down the stairs in a purple sundress I had just bought.

"You look beautiful, honey," she said,

opening the door. "Hi, Jason, come on in." She gave him a quick hug.

"Wow, you look incredible, babe."

I smiled and said thank you. Truthfully, the dress was the only thing that didn't hurt to wear. I was thankful for the warm June weather, allowing me to get away with the comfort of a sundress.

"You ready to go?" he asked.

I nodded as I grabbed my bag, kissed my mom on the cheek, and headed out the door behind him. I climbed into the familiar red Sunfire with its 'new car' air freshener smell, and worn fabric seats. I put my seatbelt on and rested my bag between my feet. Jason leaned over and kissed my lips gently. When I didn't turn away, he kissed me again more passionately. The familiar butterflies washed away my unease. It was amazing how quickly he could make me forget.

The school day went quickly. It was the Friday before exam week and that left most students and teachers in a better mood. When the last bell sounded, Trish, Jason, and I grabbed our bags and headed out the front doors of the school.

"Did you hear Graham is having a party tonight?" Trish asked. Graham was the quarterback and star athlete of the school. He was known for hosting some of the best parties.

"You know my parents will never agree to that." I sighed loudly at my sheltered life. Jason wrapped his arm around me and pulled me in close.

"What if you say you're sleeping at Trish's house tonight?" he offered.

"Yes! Please!" Trish agreed, pleading with me to lie to my parents just this once. I hesitated before agreeing. She squealed and hugged me.

"Come over at 7:00 p.m. and we will get ready, ok? Jason, can you drive?" she asked, looking in his direction.

"Of course, anything for my girl and her bestie," he said, kissing the top of my head. Trish smiled wide and then caught her bus home.

Jason pulled up to my house and put the car in park. He turned to look at me. His blue eyes focused on where he had hit me.

"How are you doing?" he asked.

I looked at him and put on my brave smile. "I'm okay."

"Does it hurt?"

Yes … I wanted to say.

"Only a little," I lied.

"Let me see it," he said.

27

I shook my head no and told him I was okay. He insisted again and I didn't want to upset him. Carefully I lifted my dress, suddenly aware of how vulnerable I was with my underwear exposed. His hand reached out to touch the purple-and-blue bruise, and then travelled down my thigh where it rested. Slowly, I pulled my dress back down.

"I'm so sorry," he said again, his head against the steering wheel. "I don't deserve you. I'm such a jerk."

I don't know why I chose this moment to defend him, but some trigger went off in my head that made me reach for him and take his hand. I turned his face to mine and saw the anguish in his eyes, and for some reason my heart ached to comfort him.

"I love you." The words were out before I could take them back. The pain in his eyes softened to that of love once more and he smiled.

"Really?" he asked.

"Yes," I said. The sad part was that I meant it. I did love him. I loved him even though I knew it was wrong.

"I love you too," he said.

CHAPTER SEVEN

Trish and I stood outside her house waiting for Jason to pick us up for the party. We were dressed in black dresses—Trish's, of course—that barely covered my thighs. I found myself frequently pulling at the hem of the dress in a futile attempt to create length where it didn't exist.

"Are you sure these aren't too short?" I said as I continued to pull on the dress. Trish raised her eyebrows at me and shook her head.

"Would you stop it already. You look hot! Wait until Jason sees you. He won't want to let you out of his sight tonight."

I smiled at her comment. My hair fell in loose curls down my back, and Trish had given me a make-over with the smoky-eye effect. I felt confident that I looked good, but I couldn't shake off the underlying unease.

Jason pulled up at 9:30 p.m. and honked his horn twice at us while whistling. Trish laughed, and I blushed nervously as we climbed into his car.

"You ladies look great!" he said, putting the car into drive and speeding off down the street. Trish gave directions from the back seat, while I sat shotgun with Jason's hand firmly on my thigh.

Graham lived outside of town in the middle of nowhere, which allowed for plenty of uninterrupted noise and mischief. The party was already packed by the time we arrived, and Trish excitedly held onto my arm as she dragged me towards the open door and away from Jason. I looked back at him, mouthing a silent sorry. He nodded his head, giving me a small smile.

"Oh my goodness! Do you see all these hot guys? It's awesome!" Trish exclaimed as she made flirty eyes with every guy who walked past us. Eventually, we found the kitchen where the keg of beer sat with a stack of plastic cups beside it. Trish grabbed two and handed me one. I hesitated when she finished filling hers with beer. She gave me the 'don't make me drink alone face'. I rolled my eyes and filled my cup.

The music blasted as we weaved through the crowd of already intoxicated couples making out. I found myself nervously searching for Jason, hoping he wasn't too upset that Trish had taken most of my attention.

"Dance with me!" Trish yelled, stopping us in the middle of the living room.

"What?" I yelled back, her words only a muffle next to the music. She grabbed my hips and started moving us, signaling that she wanted us to dance. I smiled, tipped my cup back and finished the rest of my beer before moving my hips and dancing. This was fun. I was glad I decided to go out. Trish and I rarely got any girl time. I was thankful Jason seemed to be understanding.

We were filling up our fourth cup of beer, and taking a break from dancing when I excused myself from Trish and stepped out back for some fresh air and a bit of quiet. I was definitely feeling unsteady and slightly dizzy. I'd never really drank or been drunk before and I wasn't so sure I liked the feeling. The door opened and Jason walked out and leaned against the house.

"Hey you, I was looking everywhere for you."

"Sorry, Trish had us dancing the night away." I smiled at him and took a sip of my beer. He smiled and moved in front of me so that my back was pressed against the cool brick of the house. It felt nice against my flushed skin. His arms were braced on either side of my head, his lips inches from mine. I could smell whiskey on his breath. He was supposed to drive us back to Trish's house later.

"How are you feeling?" he asked, tucking a curl behind my ear. I bit my lip and looked up at him.

"Honestly, a little dizzy and wobbly," I said, half laughing. He laughed and grazed his thumb across my lips.

"That means you're drunk, babe. Enjoy it." He kissed me then, his lips pressing hard against mine as his hands grabbed my hair and pulled it playfully. The kiss deepened, awakening a warmth within me that I had never experienced before. My head felt like it was floating, and his kisses on my neck were better than usual. I moaned softly as he nibbled my ear.

"I want to make you mine," he whispered in my ear. My body tensed and I stumbled backwards and looked at him with wide eyes. His hands were on my hips, pulling me against the obvious hardness in his jeans.

"Jason–" His finger pressed against my lips, silencing me mid-sentence. He leaned down and gently kissed my lips.

"I know you're a virgin, babe, it's okay. Let me be your first. You love me, right?" He was saying each word between soft kisses on my lips.

"Of course I love you, but–" Again his finger pressed against my lips.

"That's what couples do when they love each other. They give themselves to one another completely."

I swallowed the lump in my throat. I wasn't ready for this. I'd had too much to drink and we were hardly somewhere romantic. His hand was on my thigh, slowly travelling upwards until it rested on my hip ... beneath my dress. I squirmed against his grip.

"Jason, you're hurting me," I whispered as he held me tightly against him. His face wasn't that of a loving boyfriend anymore; he glared at me as if I were a possession, a prize to be won no matter the cost.

"I don't want to do this. I'm not ready."

I tried to push him back, but his other hand came fast around my throat, pinning me against the wall. I gasped, unable to scream, and hardly able to catch a breath against his strength. His free hand slid from my hip until it reached my breast. I closed my eyes as tears slid down my cheeks.

"You're so beautiful," he whispered in my ear, loosening his grip on my neck, but not removing his hand.

He kept busy violating my body while I stood there pinned, praying for someone to come outside and stop him. I couldn't believe this was happening. Was my boyfriend going to rape me out here? Was Jason really that cruel?

His lips were on mine again; his tongue invading my mouth, as the whiskey on his breath claimed my senses. He turned me around so that I was pinned face-first against the bricks. My heart hammered painfully in my chest. *Oh god, please no.*

"Jason, please, not like this!" I wanted to scream it, but my voice was barely a whisper.

"I love you," was all he said before ripping off my underwear and taking away my innocence. I tried to cry out, but his hand came over my mouth to quiet me.

Silently, with tears soaking my cheeks, he raped me. When it was over, he turned me around, wiped the mascara stains from my face, kissed my forehead, and once again told me he loved me.

I sunk to the ground against the wall after he went back into the party, my body trembling. Reaching across the grass, I grabbed my underwear, shakily putting them back on and wiped my tears. I thought about what had just happened. *Did he rape me?* I couldn't make sense of it all. Was it considered rape if you were together? He had said that it was what couples did when they loved each other, and he loved me.

My brain worked to formulate a reason, or as I later realized to be an excuse as to what Jason had done to me. He loved me so much that he wanted to be connected the only way possible in a relationship. He didn't rape me; it was my first time, so it was supposed to be unenjoyable. At least that's what I made myself believe.

I stood up and straightened my dress, smoothed my hair with my fingers, wiped my cheeks, and put that fake smile that I'd come to know so well back on my face.

CHAPTER EIGHT

It was Saturday afternoon when I hugged Trish goodbye and headed down the sidewalk. I had one destination in mind: the pharmacy. 'Al's Pharmacy' was only a short walk away from Trish's house. I found myself walking at a brisk pace, feeling the need to get there as soon as possible.

When I arrived, my eyes scanned the shelves of the aisle, but I couldn't see it anywhere. With burning embarrassment, I approached the pharmacist counter.

"How can I help you, miss?" the cashier said.

"I'm looking for the *Plan B* pill," I murmured, feeling the heat in my cheeks. The cashier smiled at me and told me to wait just a moment before he headed over to speak with the pharmacist. I saw him walk down an aisle, reach to the top shelf and pull the tiniest 'I made the biggest mistake of my life' box down off the shelf.

He walked over and handed the little box of mistakes to me.

"This has to be taken within seventy-two hours to be effective," he instructed.

I nodded quickly, wanting to get the hell out of there.

"Do you have any questions?" he asked.

I shook my head and quickly paid the cashier, nearly running out of the store. As I walked down the sidewalk, I tore open the box and removed the little pill. I popped it onto my tongue and swallowed, feeling it move down my dry throat and hopefully working its magic.

I wasn't on any birth control because I'd never been sexually active before. I kicked myself now for my lack of preparedness.

You didn't ask to be sexually active; it was forced on you, a little voice in my head reminded me. I silently told it to shut up. I threw the box into a nearby bush to hide the evidence from my parents and quickly squashed the negative thoughts in my head. *He loves you,* I told myself over and over until I reached my house and believed once again that Jason was the greatest thing in my life. The day travelled by slowly, my mind a blur of drunken images. I was lying on my bed when a text message came in.

> *Jason: Hey, babe, miss you, you ok? You've been quiet.*

I stared at his text message as I lay on my bed. He truly doesn't see a problem with last night, so why should I?

> *Amy: I miss you too. I'm ok, a bit sore today tho.*

I pressed send, waiting to see what he would say about that, or if he'd pretend like we didn't have sex last night.

> *Jason: Don't worry, babe! That's completely normal for your first time. It will be better next time, promise.*

My skin went cold at the words *next time*. I couldn't imagine doing that again so soon. Instinctively, I crossed my legs, feeling the ache between them where he had 'made me his.'

The truth was there. Jason and I had sex last night. It hurt, it was scary, but it happened. He was my boyfriend; he took my virginity and I now completely belonged to him. I told myself to be happy about this, that it was nice to be that important to someone and to be loved. Again, I put on my brave face and texted him back.

Amy: I love you, next time will be better!

I felt the nausea in my stomach as I hit send. Maybe it would be better, more romantic and gentler than the first time. I was sure Jason had a plan to make the *next time* extra special, and so I smiled to myself. This was the moment where I should have seen how he was warping my mind, and how everything was wrong. Instead, I chose to see the caring boyfriend who promised me it wouldn't hurt, and the weak version of myself believed him.

CHAPTER NINE

The next few weeks flew by as the weather got warmer, the days got longer, and the school year came to an end. Jason had continued to be the perfect boyfriend ever since that night and I found myself forgetting that awful memory. My heart still did little summersaults whenever he walked into the room, and my eyes lit up when he would put his arm around me and say, 'How's my girl?' Truth be told, I loved being 'His girl.' 'Jason's girl.' The 'lucky' girl.

Trish started dating the captain of the basketball team and that led to double dates. It was nice to be able to do things together. I never worried about Jason's mood when we were with Trish and her boyfriend, and he never felt threatened for my attention; he was just the sweet guy I loved.

Our three-month anniversary was today and Jason had been promising me a romantic night for the last week to celebrate. When the last bell sounded and school was out for the summer, he wrapped his arm around my waist and pulled me against him at my locker, kissing me softly.

"Ready for tonight, beautiful?" His eyes were super blue today and were drinking me in like I was the most precious thing on this earth.

"You bet. I'm so curious about what you have planned!" My heart raced when he leaned down and whispered into my ear.

"I'm going to make you mine again, on a blanket under the stars." He kissed me again, nibbling my lower lip before grazing my tongue with his.

"Are you ready for that?" he asked.

"I'm ready," I said breathlessly, his warm lips still pressed against mine. I was ready this time, excited even. This was how it should be, romantic and gentle.

Jason picked me up at 8:30 p.m. I climbed into his car, wearing my jean shorts and tank top. I gave him a kiss on the cheek as I buckled my seatbelt. He reached into the back seat and handed me a bouquet of red roses. I smiled widely as I took them from him.

"You're so sweet!" I was so in love with him at that very moment that it almost physically hurt. I couldn't imagine my life without Jason. I didn't want to. He leaned over and kissed me deeply, our tongues teasing each other, intensity growing. He pulled back, laughing.

"You better let me drive to our spot or I'll ravish you right here in this car!" He backed the Sunfire out onto the road and I smiled as his hand took its place on my thigh. I loved car rides with him and the way he always touched me in some way.

We arrived at the same open field with the old swing set that had come to be 'our' special place. He came around and opened my door, helping me out. From the trunk he grabbed a blanket, a bottle of wine, and an old radio.

"I'm going to make sure this is a night you will never forget," he promised as we walked to the clearing.

I helped him lay the blanket out and we sat side by side just as the sun was setting. He popped open the wine bottle and poured us each a glass. I guzzled mine, wanting to have some liquid courage for when we had sex again. After the third glass, I was feeling buzzed and giddy. I was laughing at every silly joke he told me and leaning into him more and more. The stars had replaced the sunset and I found myself on my back gazing into his eyes, seeing the lust in them.

"I want you," he said.

"Take me," I replied, finding courage and a desire in me that I didn't know existed. I silently thanked the empty bottle of wine that had rolled off the blanket. Jason leaned over me and slowly pulled down my shorts and tank top. With little effort he had my bra off and I was completely naked and vulnerable beneath him.

"You're perfect," he said, trailing a finger from my lips, down my neck, and between my breasts until he was at my hips. I breathed deeply, anticipation propelling my need. He slid his jeans off and looked me in the eyes. "Ready?"

I nodded and he slid into me. My fingers dug into his shoulders as he pushed deeper. I gasped and he smoothed my hair to soothe me. As he started to move and quicken his pace, I found myself crying out with every thrust. He didn't seem to notice, he just continued harder and harder.

"Jason, it's hurting," I said, tears welling in my eyes.

He stopped for a second and looked down at me, kissing my lips gently, his tongue exploring my mouth. "It's okay, babe, you're doing great. The more you relax and the more we do this, the better it will feel for you."

He moved again and this time I kept quiet. I shut my eyes and mentally tried to relax. I was never going to 'get good' at it if I just kept complaining about how it hurt all the time. It wasn't all bad, it did feel nice when he was gentle, however his gentle moments were far and few between. Once he was finished, he pulled out and rolled off of me, all sweaty and satisfied. I lay there still naked and aching.

I sat up and stretched for my clothes. His eyes glared at me with silent warning.

"Don't," he said.

My brows furrowed together with confusion, as I shivered from the chill that had settled in for the night. "I'm cold."

Again, I reached for my clothes. He grabbed my wrist tightly and yanked me back onto the blanket.

"Ow, Jason, that hurts. Let go of me!" I drew my arm back, but his grip tightened painfully.

"I'm not done with you yet, Amy. It's our anniversary, you owe me this. I even got you flowers."

I stared at him, my wrist still clutched in his hand. There was no way I could handle more right now. It hurt enough already. He was glaring at me with accusatory eyes, daring me to say 'no' to what he wanted on this 'special' day.

"Lie on your stomach this time."

I did as he said, and I wept through the whole thing until he once again rolled off of me. When I stood up, blood trickled down my inner thigh and pain coursed through my body. I fervently dressed before sitting down beside him.

"Thank you," I said, afraid that if I showed even the slightest shred of ungratefulness for tonight that he would hurt me again.

CHAPTER TEN

It was 11:02 p.m. when I crawled into my bed and wrapped the blankets around me as tight as they would go. I was shivering, though I knew it wasn't from being cold. My mind replayed the night over and over until the memory burned like acid through my veins. I felt violated, ashamed, and completely helpless. I was torn between confiding in my mom or Trish, but worried about never getting to see him again. *Pathetic, right?* After everything that happened, I still didn't want to lose him. A small part of me believed there was good in him, that he really did love me, even if he didn't always know how to express it.

I clicked on my bedside lamp and looked at my wrist where he had grabbed me; it was red, and the marks of his fingers wrapped around like a bruise, claiming yet another part of me. I massaged it as I closed my eyes and wept into my pillow.

∞ ∞ ∞

I wish I could say that things got better; that I could put the past behind me and forget about it. I was wrong. Jason was the perfect gentleman everywhere we went; he held doors open for me, cleared the dishes after dinner with my parents, and always had me back home before curfew. The truth is, Jason saved his anger and his lash outs for when no one was around. The sound of a door closing behind us was all he needed to unleash his frustrations and leave his mark hidden beneath my clothing. It's sad to say, but I started to get used to him hitting, pinching, and slapping me. The bruises and marks eventually faded before being replaced with fresh ones. My parents were never the wiser. They loved everything about him; they didn't know the tormented side of him. While the bruises would hurt for a little while, I still preferred it over him forcing himself on me which thankfully hadn't happened for a few weeks.

I wasn't scared of him so much as I was numb to it all. It's like a little switch inside my brain turned off in an attempt to save the smallest shred of the girl I used to be. I still loved Jason, the twisted part of my heart excusing his behavior for the struggles he was facing. His parents were divorcing after twenty-seven years, his older brother moved out, and all his life he watched his dad beat on his mom;

it had become an acceptable, normal behavior to him. *He doesn't know any better* is what I would tell myself each time he hurt me.

After he would finish lashing out, his gentle side would return and I'd find myself in his arms, my head resting on his chest as I listened to his heart rate slow and his demons fade away. This was when I loved him the most; his love was the strongest right after an episode and he would tell me how amazing I was, and how lucky he was to have me. I believed every word, every time; that was until the next time, and what should have been the last time.

August hung thick and heavy in the air, its intense heat yellowing the once-green grass. I knew something was wrong when I saw Jason speeding around the corner and screeching to a stop in front of my house. It was Saturday afternoon and I was home alone. He had gotten out of his car, leaving the door ajar and rushed over to me, his breathing rapid and heavy, his anger nearly palpable. I remember cautiously stepping back and asking what was wrong. Across the street, my neighbor, Mr. Jenkins, was watering his lawn and I wondered whether Jason had noticed that he had an audience. He was yelling at me now, his face red and his fists clenched against his sides. He was screaming about how much he hated his dad, about what a piece of shit he was and how he wanted to kill him for hurting his mom for years.

Mr. Jenkins had stopped watering the grass and was watching with concern from across the road. I darted my eyes between the two of them, and gently touched Jason's arm, urging him to calm down. That was a huge mistake. Within moments, he had me pinned against the house, his hands gripping my shirt and slamming me against the wall over and over, my head hitting the brick with every shake.

I could hear my neighbor shouting something, but I was too dizzy to comprehend. Jason stopped, and his fists took over, colliding into my ribs. I counted each time as it took my breath away and knocked me to my knees. *One ... two ... three ... four ...* It wasn't until the fifth strike and I was on the ground that he climbed on top of me, one hand pinning me to the ground by my hair, while punching me repeatedly in the face with the other. I could feel my consciousness slipping away with every blow to my head, and within moments there was nothing but darkness.

CHAPTER ELEVEN

My mind tried to swim through the darkness, scrambling to reach the surface. I could hear muffled beeping of a machine as if from the end of a long tunnel. I tried to open my eyes, but with so much swelling my vision was a blur. The metallic taste of dried blood coated my tongue and instantly images of Jason's attack flooded my brain. I could feel his fingers tightening around my throat, his fist knocking the wind out of me with every strike, and the venom in his words as his rage left me in a helpless, beaten pile on my front yard. Tears left traces down my cheeks as I wondered how I had gotten to this state, and mourned the loss of the parts of me I could never get back.

"Mom?" It was a whisper, but it was

enough to get her attention. She was beside my bed, her eyes closed and her body slumped in a small chair. She looked at me, tears in her eyes, and reached for my hand, tightly squeezing it.

"Hi, sweetie," she said softly as she brushed the hair from my face. She smiled at me, not a happy smile, of course, but a smile thanking God that I was still alive. I silently thanked Him too.

I glanced around the room and took note of the machine I had heard, the intravenous in my hand steadily hydrating me with every beep. Wires trailed from my chest to a screen beside my bed, displaying my vitals, and a nurse sat just outside my room, writing notes in my chart. She looked up to see that I was awake and made her way over to me. Her badge was blurry, but I made out three simple letters: ICU. My heart beat faster as the shock of just how badly I was hurt sunk in. I was in intensive care and Jason ... where was Jason?

"My name's Kimmy," the nurse said as she pulled out her stethoscope and placed it on my chest. "How are you feeling, Amy? How is your pain?" she continued, moving the stethoscope across my chest.

I tried to speak but my mouth was so dry it felt like cotton. Nurse Kimmy smiled at me and said she'd be back with some water and pain medication. My mom stood there holding my hand. I could see the questions burning on her lips, desperate to ask but trying to remain patient.

After a few minutes, the nurse returned with some water and a tiny cup with two green pills. She placed the straw to my lips and I sipped eagerly, the contents of the cup nearly draining in seconds. She then held the tiny cup of pills to my lips and told me it was morphine and would help keep me comfortable. I let her tip the meds into my mouth before I finished off the rest of the water and smiled at her gratefully.

"Where's Jason?" I managed to ask as my dad entered the room with two cups of coffee. He smiled at me and handed the cups to Mom as he leaned over and kissed me on the cheek.

"Hey, kiddo, it's nice to see you awake." He grabbed his coffee from Mom and took a small sip, taking her hand in his and giving it a gentle squeeze. My heart ached at the pain on their faces. Was it really that bad? I suddenly wished desperately for a mirror.

"Where's Jason?" I repeated, darting my eyes between my parents. My dad took a deep breath before answering.

"He's in jail, honey. He can't hurt you

anymore. You're safe." My dad smiled at me as if the thought of Jason being in jail was enough to erase the fear and panic that coursed through my veins.

"If it wasn't for Mr. Jenkins witnessing the whole thing and calling the police, who knows what would have happened." My mom's voice shook, fighting back her tears.

"How bad is it?" I found myself asking, afraid of the answer.

My mom looked at my dad and then at me, her hand wrapped tightly around her untouched coffee.

"You were hurt pretty badly, Amy. He broke four of your ribs, gave you two black eyes, internal bleeding, and a concussion."

She was crying now, her body shaking with each breath she took. My dad pulled her against him and kissed the top of her head. I was crying too, but not because of the injuries, and not because my parents were a mess, but because I was about to say something so completely screwed up that I really must have had a concussion.

"I want to see him," I said, my eyes fixed on the wall in front of my bed. I didn't dare look for their reactions; I knew how absurd I sounded.

"Not a chance in hell," my dad said, unable

to disguise the anger and hatred he felt for Jason.

I turned to look at him; his eyes were fixed on mine.

"I still love him." They were four words that creeped off my tongue and slapped my parents directly in the face. They stared at me in shock, wondering how their daughter could still love the monster who had put her into the Intensive Care Unit. It was at that moment I learned just how blind love can make you. I was still completely, stupidly, and irrevocably in love with my boyfriend, my abuser, my everything. Despite the physical injuries, there was a shred of naïve hope that desperately clung to the good parts of him, the parts that didn't exist but I continued to keep alive through memories so tainted they could hardly be trusted.

Yes, I was afraid of Jason, but I was even more afraid of losing him.

CHAPTER TWELVE

The next few days passed slowly. At this point, I had seen the state of my injuries when I had gotten up to go to the bathroom. The bruising on my face was tough to see at first, but eventually lost its shock factor as the days passed.

My mom never left my side for more than an hour or so to go home and shower, and my dad kept himself busy with work and visiting me in the hospital. With all the commotion of the last week, I was desperate for a moment to myself to process what had happened. After one week in the ICU, I was finally given the green light to go home.

Everything was exactly as it was before the incident, yet nothing felt the same, or perhaps I just wasn't the same. I walked up the stairs to my room and closed the door behind me. Sitting down on the floor, I put my back against the door and looked around my room; this was my sanctuary, my room of dreams and mistakes, of sleepless nights and unforgettable memories. I closed my eyes and breathed slowly, feeling my ribs ache against my bandages. Jason flooded my mind, and memories of our stolen kisses and quiet moments filled the room.

God, I missed him. I missed him and I hated him and I loved him. *Why do I still love him?* I cried again; an ugly, silent cry that painfully shook my body. I knew he didn't deserve my love, I knew it was wrong on nearly every spectrum, but I couldn't shut those feelings off. I couldn't just erase how he made me feel in those moments where he was tender and sweet. The truth was, the girl who existed before Jason, didn't exist anymore; she was gone. The new girl, the new me, didn't know how to go on without the person who had become such a big part of my life.

"Honey, are you okay?" My mom knocked softly on the door, her worry clear in her voice.

I sighed loudly and pleaded with her to leave me alone. I could picture her pausing at the door, hesitating to leave her poor, broken daughter alone before walking away and heading down the stairs. I climbed onto my bed and pulled the soft blankets over me, pressed my bruised face into the pillows and wondered what he was doing in jail right now, how he was feeling, if he was okay, and whether he missed me as much as I missed him. I also wondered if he was sorry … sorry for hurting me, sorry for damaging the love we had, or if he was sorry for leaving me alone, not knowing whether we'd ever see each other again.

I opened my nightstand drawer where my cell phone sat in the bottom right corner, shiny and inviting, beckoning to quench the curiosity that burned through me. I picked it up, the case cold in my hand as I typed in my pin and the home screen lit up. Five missed calls, two being Trish and three an unknown number. I clicked the phone off again, none of those were what I had wanted to see. I wanted his name to show up with a trail of apologetic texts that would wrap me in a tight embrace of false comfort. I wanted to talk to him again. I needed an explanation, to see his blue eyes, and hear *I'm sorry* face to face. I needed closure. I needed Jason.

CHAPTER THIRTEEN

I was an idiot of epic proportions. I stood outside the gates, my hand hovering over the intercom button as my heart raced. *What am I doing?* Elmwood County Jail was a large, depressing shade of grey brick that housed hundreds of criminals; one who just happened to be my boyfriend. I bit my lip and pushed the button. Crackling static sounded before a man's voice requested my name and purpose of visit. The gates opened and I made my way to the security clearance area. A woman with a stern face forced a smile and asked me to put my belongings in a bucket and for me to step through the body scanner.

Fifteen minutes later, I found myself sitting on a cold metal chair, staring at a plexi-glass window with a yellowed phone. I twisted my hands anxiously in my lap until I saw him. My heart lurched. He looked so different. Unkempt facial hair shadowed his face, and his eyes were a dull blue. Our eyes met and I could feel myself wanting to cry. He picked up the phone on his side, and shakily I reached for mine.

"Amy …" His voice was nearly a whisper, full of remorse and heartache. The lump in my throat swelled until tears escaped down my cheeks. I put my hand against the glass.

"Jason …" He put his hand against mine on the other side of the window and I imagined the warmth of his skin against mine.

"I'm so sorry, babe. I don't know what happened. I just lost it. I …" His voice cracked and I was shaking my head, telling him it's okay, comforting him.

"Do you forgive me? I love you so much." He looked at me with sad blue eyes and I looked back, deeply searching for what was truth and what was lies. The real truth was that I had absolutely no idea what to believe. All I knew was that I loved him, and it killed me to see him this way. This is the part of my story where I should have learned to never go back to what broke me; that he didn't deserve me and he was a monster. Instead, I nodded and agreed to forgive him.

The one-minute warning for time being up

sounded and we stood up and put the phones back on their hooks. A corrections officer took hold of his arm to lead him back to his cell. Jason looked back and mouthed *I love you* before disappearing around the corner.

I stood there for a moment longer, glued to the image of his orange jumpsuit and imprisonment before I turned and made my way out of the jail. I knew once my parents discovered the car gone and found out where I had went that I would be in big trouble, from dad especially. They just didn't understand the connection that Jason and I have; we complete each other and for him to be locked away not only hurts him, but it breaks my own heart, too. I could tell he was sorry for hurting me. It was written all over his face. If that was enough for me then why couldn't it be enough for them?

I pulled the car into the driveway and put it into park. A black police cruiser occupied the other half of the driveway, and panic set in about where I had just been. I wasn't even sure if that was allowed or not. When I opened the front door, I found the three of them sitting at the kitchen table, each one turned to look my way.

"Where were you?" Dad asked, a serious expression clouding his usually bright brown eyes.

"Just out for a drive," I replied, awkwardly shifting back and forth under everyone's scrutiny.

Mom was biting her nails, a nervous habit that usually meant she was extremely worried or stressed. My eyes met hers and she quickly looked away as the police officer pulled out some papers and cleared his throat.

"Hi, Amy. My name is Detective Thompson. I need to go over some details, get a statement, and have you sign some papers to press formal charges against Jason." He pulled out his pen and clicked it open, the papers waiting for me to make my move. I looked from him to my parents and took a deep breath because what I was about to say was the biggest mistake I ever could have made.

"I don't want to press charges."

CHAPTER FOURTEEN

Detective Thompson pushed his chair back from the table, the wooden legs grinding against the tile floor. He cleared his throat and fixed his attention on me. I stood with my arms crossed and my face determined; this was my choice and I wasn't about to budge.

"Amy, based on the seriousness and nature of your injuries, Jason will be charged with domestic assault, regardless of your wish to not press charges. He committed a serious crime and put you in the ICU. He needs to be held accountable for his actions."

Tears were ruining the act of toughness I had been portraying. I was confused, frustrated, and angry. Where were my options? My choices? Didn't I have a say in what happened? My hands were in fists and my chest heaved with the effort to keep myself together. Mom came over to me and tried to wrap her arms around me, but I quickly moved away.

"Don't!" I shouted. "Everyone just leave me alone. I'm not some broken little girl. Why don't I have any choices in this? I don't want to be a victim. I want to be with Jason!"

I realized that I was being irrational and that I didn't make sense. How could they know how I was feeling? They had no idea how I felt about Jason or how much he loved me. He made a mistake and everyone was acting like it was the end of the world. I was sick and tired of being told what to do or how I should feel. The room suddenly felt like a hundred degrees, the walls feeling too close together, and the air too thick. I excused myself and walked out onto the porch where the summer sun cast warmth across my face and birds chirped care free in the sky. I silently cursed them for their simple lives.

"May I join you?" Detective Thompson stepped onto the porch and closed the door. I shrugged and looked away. He stood beside me, arms resting on the rail and eyes searching the sky, a small smile on his face.

"It's a blessing to enjoy days like today," he started, turning to look at me. "You are lucky to be alive and standing here beside me, Amy. The brutality of what Jason did to you was horrific. Your neighbor saved your life by witnessing the attack and calling the police."

I rolled my eyes and started to turn away when his hand rested on top of mine.

"Wait, please. I know you're confused, lost, and hurting, and you feel like you have no one to turn to, no one but Jason. In your mind, he is the only one who understands you and cares about you, correct?"

I was fixated on my hands, tears sliding down my cheeks. I didn't want to admit how right he was, and how wrong I was for feeling that way.

"It is completely natural for a victim of domestic assault to want to protect the abuser, and to recant or withhold statements and details in an attempt to lessen the severity of a crime. I'm really hoping you stand up for yourself and come to terms with just how bad this could have turned out before deciding to forgive and forget the events that took place. Bruising may fade and bones may heal, but the scars that run deep from this will always be on the surface to remind you that Jason is a dangerous man. You have parents in there who love you and just went through the worst ordeal of their lives, nearly losing their child at the hands of the person they trusted to protect their little girl and whom they had invited into their home with open arms. Think about all this when you go to bed tonight. Think long and hard. Perhaps come morning everything will seem a little clearer." Detective Thompson squeezed my hand before walking down the driveway to his cruiser. He gave a wave and headed down the street.

As I was standing there, my mind in a whirl, pieced together a thousand fragments of memories, promises, text messages, and concealed bruises. I held my head in my hands as my body was wracked with silent sobbing. I had never felt more alone. How would I get through this? How was I supposed to do the right thing when, to me, being with the one who was so wrong felt so right?

CHAPTER FIFTEEN

Trish hugged me so tightly that I had to remind her my ribs were still healing. Her face was all sadness and full of best friend concern and guilt, it made my stomach twist into a bunch of little knots. We were sitting on a bench at the beach, escaping the scrutiny of my parents; Trish was the only way I was probably ever going to be allowed to leave the house alone again.

"I can't believe I didn't see the signs." Trish picked at her nail polish, lost in her own thoughts.

I sighed, defeated, and took her hand. "Please don't blame yourself, Trish. Really … I'm okay. No one could have known that this was coming."

She looked at me with tears in her eyes

and squeezed my hand tightly.

"Are you really okay? Because it's okay to not be, you know? You don't have to be so strong all the time. I'm here for you, Amy."

I smiled at her weakly and shook my head.

"I'm confused, but I'm okay." That was probably the most honest thing I had admitted in a while. She looked at me then, concern in her eyes.

"What are you confused about?"

I wasn't sure how or if I should answer her question honestly. Trish was my best friend, and I had faith that I could tell her anything.

"I still love him, Trish. I love him with every broken part of me, and it kills me to know he's locked away." I held my breath, waiting for the explosion of comments about how stupid I was, but she just sat there quietly, thinking.

"I get that," she said, much to my surprise.

"I mean, he put on an amazing show. He had everyone fooled. I don't believe that was all an act though. Despite all the horrid recent events, I am sure there are some good parts to him deep down."

Trish gave my hand a reassuring squeeze and pulled me in for a long hug.

"I'm so glad you're still here with me. Don't ever scare me like that again. Got it?"

I laughed and nodded in agreement.

"Have you heard anything about it all? My parents have me banned from the news and reality."

"It was on the news after it happened. They interviewed your neighbor who witnessed it and called the police. He had described it as horrific and senseless. Reporters who were on the scene quickly showed some footage of Jason in handcuffs. He looked distraught," Trish explained, watching my reaction.

"I need to see him, Trish, at least one more time. I need to know why, face to face. I want to feel his arms around me one more time and remember what it felt like to be normal again."

"The only way I can see that happening is if he makes bail, and even then there's no way you will be able to go anywhere with him. Between your parents, reporters, and most likely some type of restraining order, it will be next to impossible."

I looked away, my mind trying to formulate a plan. I would have to breech the restraining order if it came down to that. We would have to find a way, no matter what.

"Can I at least ask one thing if you decide to go all crazy and see him?" Trish asked.

I nodded and waited.

"Text me whenever you are going to sneak out to see him. Tell me where and when, and tell me when you're home again after, so I know you're safe … please?"

"Of course, Trish, but you have to promise to keep this secret, no matter what."

She nodded, promising to stay quiet. We walked back to my house where she hugged me goodbye and said she would text me later. I waved and started to walk towards the front door. I heard the sound of footsteps behind me and I turned. My breath caught in my throat as a skinny man with a balding head stuck his video camera in my face.

"How do you feel since the attack, Miss Andrews? Have you made a full recovery? Do you still love him? What's in your future now that Jason is locked away?"

I stood there with my mouth open, frozen to the spot, my heart hammering. Who did he think he was?

"Get out of here! Leave now or I'll call the police," my dad shouted, running across the front lawn and wrapping his arm around me. He led us away from the reporter and into the house.

"Are you okay?" he asked, full of concern.

I nodded and peeked out the window. The man was walking away with his camera at his side.

"Filthy reporters. They have no respect,"

Dad muttered as he walked back into the living room and resumed his show.

I headed up to my bedroom and shut the door, climbed onto my bed, and pulled out my cell phone. My fingers scrolled to Jason's name and his last text message to me.

Jason: Good morning, angel, I miss you, see you later for our date! ☺

The memories flashed again. He had shown up angry and volatile, far from the mood he was in when talking about our date. I wondered what we would have done had he not shown up so angry and violent. I pictured us back in our special spot at the park, his lips on mine, soft and sweet. It was easy to forget the times he pushed me too far with sex, because at this very moment I craved that connection with him; I longed to feel close to him like that again.

I knew he was locked away in a prison cell, with no mean to his cell phone, but my fingers took over and messaged him anyways in a desperate attempt to make contact.

Amy: I know you can't see this right now, and I'm probably crazy for reaching out to you, but I wanted to tell you that I miss you so much. Please come back 2 me…

I hit send, initiating yet another mistake

that I could not come back from. Jason truly would be my undoing.

CHAPTER SIXTEEN

Two weeks passed when Detective Thompson gave news of Jason's bail. I tried my best to act concerned and quiet about it, but inside my heart was racing and my stomach flip-flopping with excitement. This was the moment I had been waiting for.

"There are some things we have to go over," Detective Thompson was saying to my parents and me. He pulled out some papers and spread them across the coffee table.

"In regards to Amy's safety, now that Jason will no longer be in prison and we await a trial, there will be a restraining order in place." He looked at me, his face serious.

"Amy, this restraining order states that Jason may not come to your home, your school, your place of work or within a set amount of kilometers from where you are at all times. If he disobeys this order then you just have to call and get to a safe place. The police will arrest him. Does that make sense so far?"

I nodded and bit my lower lip, my mind imagining every possible way to break this restraining order and be with Jason again.

"It is important that you don't give in to temptation or try to reach out to him, Amy, no matter how badly you want to. He is a dangerous man. Remember that. The police and your family are relying on you to obey this order just as much as we are relying on Jason to, understood?"

"Yes," I lied.

"Good, now according to the county jail, Jason will be released this afternoon and escorted by police back home to his parents. I will call with any updates, and please don't hesitate to call me with any concerns." He looked at me as he said this. His eyes held mine as if he knew what I was thinking. I swallowed the lump in my throat and promised to call him if I felt in danger. He gave me his card once again, and I tucked it into my back pocket to add to the others stashed in my bedside table.

∞ ∞ ∞

Amy: Did you hear? Jason's getting out

on bail this afternoon!!!
Trish: No way! What are you planning??
Amy: I'm not sure yet … I texted him two
weeks ago, hoping he will get his cell
phone and reach out to me … there's a
restraining order in place like you had
mentioned there might be. I guess I wait
to see if he replies?
Trish: Stay safe and remember our deal,
ok?
Amy: Promise xo
Trish: Love U
Amy: Love U 2

I waited all day for his message and received none. I picked away at my dinner, my appetite nonexistent. My parents watched me with concern, attributing my mood to being worried that Jason was out, when in reality I was hurt because he hadn't reached out to me. Stupid, right?

"May I be excused?" I asked as I pushed my plate away.

"Of course, sweetie. Is everything okay?" Mom asked.

"Yeah, I'm fine, Mom. Just feeling tired, that's all." She smiled at me as I stood up. "Goodnight, guys. Love you."

"Love you too, honey," Dad said, and started talking to Mom about her day. I headed upstairs to my room, and sat on the edge of my bed. I was so frustrated and confused. Why wasn't he answering me? He said he still loved me when I saw him at the jail …

Hours passed and I fell asleep across my bed, my clothes still on and my phone in my hand.

Ding, ding …

The sound of a text message woke me and I quickly looked at the time. 1:15 a.m. I checked the home screen and my heart pounded harder; it was Jason.

> *Jason: Hey babe, I got your msg. Sorry it took so long to reply, I don't have a lot of privacy right now. I miss you so much xox*
>
> *Amy: Jason! I am so happy you replied. I thought you were mad at me or something … I miss you, I love you!*
>
> *Jason: Can I see you??*
>
> *Amy: I'll do anything! How do we do this without getting caught, there's a restraining order…*
>
> *Jason: I kno, we have to stick to night time for now, be sneaky about it… are you able to meet me at the corner of Adelaide, and I can pick you up? We can go to our spot.*
>
> *Amy: Yes! I'll be there in 20 mins!!!!* ☺

I couldn't believe what I was about to do. Breaking the law was never on my bucket list to success, but with Jason I seemed to have no problem throwing caution to the wind. I quickly brushed my hair and my teeth, pulled on a nicer pair of jeans and a shirt, sprayed some perfume, and snuck down the stairs. I decided to go out the back door, saving the loud squeak that the front door tended to give. Slowly, I closed the sliding glass door and ventured out into the quiet darkness. Trish's deal popped into my mind and I quickly pulled my phone out to text her as promised. My pulse quickened as I approached the corner of Adelaide. His red car sat there with its lights off, waiting. Waiting for me. God I missed him.

I opened the car door and climbed in, the familiar smell of his aftershave taking me back to better times. He was in shadows but I didn't care. I remembered his face so vividly that I didn't need any light to know who I was looking at. His hand reached out and stroked my cheek. My breath caught in my chest at his touch. I felt his lips against my forehead, warm and gentle. He pulled away and started the car, heading to our special spot.

No words were said on the drive, but his hand came to rest on my thigh like it always did, and gently he squeezed it, the warmth from his touch travelling through my entire body. Everything felt so right and I willed time to stand still. He pulled into the park, the trees becoming the cover that we needed. Jason pulled out the same blanket we always used from the trunk, and a flashlight. He came around and took my hand, guiding us to the grass. I was shaking with anticipation as he spread out the blanket. I knew what was about to come and I had never wanted it more.

"Come here, beautiful girl," he said, signaling for me to sit on his lap. I smiled and sat down. The glow of the flashlight illuminated his face and he was looking at me so thoughtfully that it made me blush.

"I missed you so much, Amy. You have no idea what kind of hell I have been through." He was stroking my hair, my body easily melting into his with every touch.

"I missed you, too. I never stopped loving you, Jason."

"Are you okay? I never meant to hurt you. I promise it will never happen again, baby." He held my face in his hands, his eyes searching mine for forgiveness.

"I'm perfect now that I'm here with you. Let's not talk about the past, please. I just want to be together in this moment right now."

Jason's lips found mine, gentle at first and

then more passionate. His hands were in my hair, stroking and pulling it, while his teeth were nibbling my lower lip. I sighed in response as his hands roamed under my shirt to my breasts. Quickly, he removed my shirt and bra and began kissing my neck and collarbone. My nails dug into his back as our bodies came alive with passion. He flipped us over so that he was on top of me, my head pressed against the soft fabric of the blanket.

"I love you, Amy," he said, his breathing heavy and his voice husky. I reached up and touched his face, tears springing to my eyes.

"I love you too, Jason," I whispered. I really did love him. Stupidly, shamefully, unconditionally loved him; just how dangerous my love for him was refused to make itself known.

We made love for what felt like hours. Jason was gentle and sweet as ever and I was tongue tied with blind faith and love. He dropped me off at the corner of Adelaide and kissed me goodbye before driving off into the early morning dawn. I crept into the house through the back door and climbed the stairs to my room. My bed felt soft and inviting as I closed my eyes and smiled. Jason was a changed man and I helplessly fell for his charm once again.

CHAPTER SEVENTEEN

The ache between my legs reminded me of last night and I smiled as I reached for my phone. I had slept in which was no surprise, considering what time I had snuck back in undetected. I could hear Mom and Dad down the hall, ranting about bills and the government and how we're all being ripped off. I unlocked the home screen on my phone to check a text from Trish.

> *Trish: How did it go?? Are you alive? TEXT ME BACK!*
>
> *Amy: Relax LOL, I am perfectly fine and made it home safe and sound early this morning. Jason was amazing. You should see how much he has changed. I think jail did him good. Haha.*
>
> *Trish: I am happy he was good to you,*

just be careful, ok? Don't let your guard down so easily…

I rolled my eyes at Trish's message and quickly typed back.

Amy: Stop worrying so much, I promise you he is different!!

Trish: I hope you are right.

"You seem to be in a good mood today," Mom said, looking up from the book she was reading.

I smiled as I poured a cup of coffee and added three heaping spoonfuls of sugar. I grabbed my cup and sat beside her on the couch, resting my head on her shoulder like I always did when I was little. She smiled and kissed the top of my head.

"It's just nice to see you smile again, honey," she said as she returned to her book and I sipped my coffee quietly beside her.

Ding, ding!

The alert of new text messages sounded on my phone where three messages arrived consecutively.

"Someone's suddenly Miss Popular," Mom teased.

I pulled my phone out to see three messages from Jason, and quickly stood up and walked to the kitchen.

Jason: I need to see you

Jason: Meet me in an hour
Jason: Same spot on the corner of Adelaide

My eyes widened at Jason's urgency, and the all-too-familiar feeling of dread twisted at my insides. I pushed it away and replied.

Amy: I can't get out right now – mom's home.

Thirty seconds later Jason replied.

Jason: Find a way.

Whoa … what was going on with him? Did something happen since last night?

Amy: Is everything ok?
Jason: I said I need to see you.
Amy: Jason, I'm not joking, there's no way for me to leave, I'm sorry.
Jason: You will be sorry if you don't meet me.

My mouth went dry at his words and my heart pounded wildly in my chest. I didn't want him to be upset with me; I wanted things to stay how they were last night. I chewed my bottom lip as I tried to come up with an excuse to sneak off alone for a bit. *Trish!* I pulled up her name on my phone and sent her a text message.

Amy: Going to meet Jason again, telling mom I'm going to your house, can you cover for me please??

Trish: Again? Didn't you just see him?
Amy: Yes but he wants to see me again,
in an hour.
Trish: He's awfully demanding. Ok. Just
this one time, you know I don't like to lie.
Amy: I owe you, love you <3
Trish: Love you too, be careful please.

"Hey, Mom?" I walked back into the living room. "That was Trish. She wants me to come for a visit and have girl time. Can I go?"

She looked up from her book once again, her brown eyes on me. "Are you planning on walking there?"

"Yes," I replied, knowing full well she wasn't going to like that answer.

"I could drive you, sweetie," she offered.

I rolled my eyes and tried to laugh lightly. "No, Mom, it's okay, really. I promise I will go straight to Trish's house," I lied.

"It's not that I don't trust you, sweetheart. I just don't–"

"Trust Jason?" I interrupted. "Mom, he's at home under watch probably from this whole damn town after what happened. Do you really think he is going to be able to walk down the street in broad daylight to come after me?" My stomach turned. I was getting way too good at lying to my mom.

She hesitated before reluctantly agreeing

to me walking to Trish's. I kissed her on the cheek and grabbed my purse as I headed out the door. I briskly walked down the road, turning to make sure that Mom didn't see me turn down the opposite street as Trish's.

Adelaide was only a few more minutes away, but I found myself picking up my pace, not wanting to be late. The corner was empty. Jason's red car wasn't idling, waiting to pick me up. I checked my watch; I was a little early. I sat down on the curb and picked at some grass jutting out between the sidewalk cracks. Footsteps stopped right behind me, and I looked up in surprise to see Jason standing over me.

"Where's your car?" I asked as I stood up. He wasn't smiling; his face was flat, giving away zero emotion.

"Too risky," he answered as he grabbed my upper arm and began to walk towards the little path between the houses where he had come from.

I squirmed in his grasp, his fingers digging painfully into my skin. "Jason, you're hurting me. What's with the death grip on my arm?"

He loosened his grip but still kept contact as we walked.

"Where are we going?" I asked, the feeling of dread once again invading my stomach. The path took us to a gravel road where his red car was parked.

"Get in," Jason ordered, holding the passenger door open.

I didn't move. My legs refused to budge as my mind worked overtime to catch up with what was happening.

"I don't want to go for a drive, Jason. Can't we just sit and talk?"

"Get in the car, Amy," he repeated sternly. I started to back up, but his grip on my arm tightened and he shoved me against the side of the car. His lips were against my ear as he dug his fingers into the skin on my arm.

"I am going to ask you one more time to get in the car before I make you get in, and trust me, you won't like it."

I winced against the pain of his grip, tears running down my cheeks. How could I have been so stupid as to think he had changed?

I climbed into the passenger seat and he slammed the door and took his seat behind the wheel. I didn't look at him. My eyes focused instead on the red marks of his fingers around my bicep. The engine started as he turned the key and put the car into drive. My pulse kept time with the metal music blasting on the radio as Jason drove down the back roads out of town.

An hour passed and we were still driving. Jason hadn't spoken a word since we left and I hadn't dared open my mouth. I chanced a glance in his direction and his blue eyes came to land on me. They didn't look angry anymore, and I breathed a sigh of relief. His one hand left the steering wheel and rested on my thigh. I cringed and fought the urge to pull away. I was so confused with my emotions.

"We're almost there, babe," he said, his soft voice returning.

"Where exactly is *there*?" I asked, looking out the window at the barren country road.

He smiled and rubbed his hand up and down my thigh. "Our new home."

My lips parted to say something but no words came out. My tongue had turned to sandpaper and my skin prickled with goosebumps. *Our new home…* What the hell was he talking about? He was still smiling at me, waiting for my response.

"But I have a home, Jason." I watched as his left hand tightened on the steering wheel, his knuckles turning white.

"Home is with me, Amy."

"Jason, you're talking crazy. Please take me home. We can't–"

His elbow collided with my temple before I could finish my sentence. Silver stars danced around as my vision blurred and I fought to hold onto reality.

"You're mine," I heard him say before the darkness took over and consciousness faded away.

CHAPTER EIGHTEEN

The pounding in my head brought me to my senses. I could feel the blood rushing in my ears as my eyes opened and what I had hoped was a nightmare became reality. The room was dimly lit from the sun shining through the dusty floral curtains, and pictures of a smiling boy and two proud parents lined the wood-paneled walls.

Oh my god. This must be the old family cottage Jason had mentioned before. He had told me it hadn't been used in years but his parents refused to sell it, not wanting to let go of the memories. *Our new home.* Jason's words replayed in my head, causing my skin to crawl with icy dread.

I sat on the side of the bed, my bare feet resting against the cool hardwood floor. Slowly,

I stood. The boards creaked beneath my weight and I held my breath, expecting his footsteps to pound down the hallway to where I was.

The house was silent and I released the air from my lungs. I walked over to the window and opened the curtains to see a large open field and rows of corn from a neighboring farm. There was nowhere close to run to, and no one to hear me scream for help. I fought back tears as I turned around and walked to the white door that held me prisoner, already knowing the answer. I jiggled the knob as if by some miracle it would be unlocked. No such luck.

A few minutes passed as I paced back and forth praying for answers before I decided to try the old bobby pin trick seen in movies. How hard could it be? I pulled one from my hair and separated the little ends before carefully inserting it into the keyhole. Slowly, I worked it in and moved it up and down as I twisted and listened for the *click* of freedom. Five minutes passed when I finally gave up and angrily threw the pin across the room. I cursed the movies for making it look so easy.

The need to escape propelled me to kick at the door full force, over and over, until my feet were red and bruised and my chest was heaving with the effort. That was when I heard the footsteps coming up the stairs, and Jason shouting. Quickly, I backed up to the far end of the room, by the window.

"What the hell, Amy! When I get in there you're going to be sorry. This is our home, you disrespectful bitch!" I flinched at his words as a key fumbled in the lock and the door swung open. His face was beet red and his hands were in white-knuckled fists.

"Jason, please … you don't have to do this."

He moved towards me in a rage. I screamed as he punched me in the ribs and brought me to my knees. I curled into a ball against the wall and tried to hide as much of my body as I could.

Jason continued to yell awful things, his words like venom going along with every blow to my body. He finally stopped a few minutes later and sat on the bed to catch his breath. Curled up against the wall as my body trembled with fear, I sobbed loudly. I wiped the blood that dripped from my lip onto my white t-shirt and tried to take a few deep breaths to calm myself. Jason looked at me then, tears pooling in his eyes as he dropped to his knees beside me and reached for my face. I flinched and he drew his hands back with a look of guilt and hurt on his face.

"I'm sorry, babe, I'm so sorry." He reached for my face again and this time I didn't cringe. I closed my eyes as his thumb wiped the blood from my lower lip and his other hand smoothed my hair back and off my tear-stained cheeks.

"I love you, Amy. You know that, right?"

I looked away from him.

"You made me mad, coming home to hear you destroying our home, to see you showing such disrespect to all the planning and work it took to be here with you ... I guess I lost it." He pulled me against his chest and I could hear his heart steadying to a normal rhythm. This used to be my favorite moment with him; this was when he was always the most loving. Now I felt like I was walking on egg shells, waiting for the next bomb to explode.

"You can't keep me here. My parents will notice I'm gone. They'll notify the police." I looked up at him, hoping he would read the urgency in my eyes. He breathed out heavily and abruptly released me as he stood up, causing me to fall back against the wall. He paced with his hands flexing between relaxed and clenched fists.

"Jason–" He held a finger up and immediately I was silenced.

"I'm thinking." His voice was clipped and cold.

"Thinking about what? They'll find you … they'll find us. This won't work."

Jason moved quickly, his fist colliding with the wall beside my head.

"Shut up!" he screamed as he pulled his fist from the hole in the wall and wiped the blood on his jeans. I squeezed my eyes shut and fought back the tears.

"Did you tell anyone that we were meeting?"

I hesitated as he waited for me to answer. There was no way he would believe me if I lied.

"Jesus, Amy, who did you tell?" He was standing in front of me with his arms crossed.

"Answer me!"

"Trish …" I managed to whisper, already anticipating him to lash out at me.

"How could you be so stupid?" His tone was cold as he sat once again on the bed in front of me. "She is going to be the reason we're found now if she opens her big mouth to your parents."

"She won't," I lied.

He laughed sarcastically and I looked down at my lap. He stood again and grabbed his car keys from his pocket.

"Well, the only option we have is to leave." I looked up at him with wide eyes. I didn't want to leave. I wanted to be found, and being here was probably my only chance.

"Leave? Where on earth would we go?"

"I can't tell you that. Now, get up." Jason dragged me to my feet and pulled out white zip-ties. He grabbed my wrists and secured them together. I winced as the plastic bit into my skin.

"Is this really necessary?" I asked as he grabbed my t-shirt and forced me to walk out of the room and down the stairs towards the front door.

"Yes, Amy, it is. I can't trust you." He buckled me into the front seat and climbed in behind the wheel.

∞∞∞

TRISH

Trish nervously stared at the incoming call on her cell phone: Amy's parents. She looked at the time. It was 8:14 p.m. and Amy was supposed to be home by now from supposedly visiting her. She chewed her fingernail, debating whether to ignore the call and keep her promise to Amy, but a voice inside her told her something wasn't right.

"Hello?" Trish answered.

"Hi, Trish. It's Monica, Amy's mom. We didn't see Amy for dinner and were wondering if she was still with you. It's getting late." Trish could hear the worry in her voice and dreaded what she was about to say.

"Listen, Mrs. Andrews, there's something you should know." There was silence on the other end as Amy's mom waited for the unpleasant news. Trish took a deep breath before coming clean.

"Amy made me promise not to say anything, but I fear she may be in trouble. She and Jason have been sneaking out to see each other, and I had been her cover. I made her promise to text me when she was meeting him and when she was back home safe, but I haven't heard anything since she went to meet him this morning. I'm so sorry. It was stupid, and I never should have supported it." More silence followed before she heard Mrs. Andrews yell in the background.

"Amy's not with Trish. She lied to us and met up with Jason. We need to phone Detective Thompson!"

The line went dead, the dial tone echoing in Trish's ear. She hung up and put her head against the cool wall as panic coursed through her for her best friend's safety.

CHAPTER NINETEEN

The station crackled as the music was abruptly cut off. Jason glanced at it annoyingly as he continued to drive down the back roads of a vacant ghost town. I stared at the speaker as a man's deep voice came over the radio.

"This is an emergency broadcast. Missing Caucasian female, eighteen years old, approximately one-hundred-and-nineteen pounds, five foot three inches, brown hair, green eyes. Last seen wearing a white t-shirt and blue jeans. Possible kidnapping. Please alert police immediately if you have any information."

My heart pounded frantically as renewed hope coursed through my veins. *They are looking for me!* I chanced a glance at Jason. The annoyed expression he wore just moments ago was replaced with rage and panic. His eyes were wide and his hands shaking as they gripped the steering wheel.

Quickly, he pulled the car over onto the dirt and shifted it into park. I panicked as he tore off his seatbelt, got out of the car and headed towards my door. I fumbled with the plastic zip-ties, trying to unbuckle my seatbelt. Jason yanked open my door, grabbed my hair and threw me onto the ground. I screamed, begging for someone to hear me as he dragged me across the dirt towards the trunk of his car.

"No, no, no! Jason, please don't! Help, somebody, please!" Tears clouded my vision as he opened the trunk and lifted me easily into it. I looked up at him with desperation, pleading for the human part of him to let me go. Instead, he looked down at me with a smirk before slamming the trunk and leaving me in darkness.

It felt like hours that I kicked and screamed, battling against the blaring music that filled the trunk. I was exhausted and soon drifted into a fretful sleep, only to be awoken by the sound of the tires crunching against gravel and the sudden halt of the car. I winced as Jason opened the trunk and grabbed my hair, forcing me to collapse from the trunk into a helpless pile at his feet. His hand stayed wrapped tightly in my hair so that my face was forced to look at him. He was still smiling in such an unrecognizable way that I found it hard to believe it had once taken my breath away.

"You're pretty when you're helpless," he said as he pulled me to my feet and backed me up against his car. His breath smelt like whiskey and cigarettes. I fought back the bile that rose in my throat as I turned away from him.

"Look at me, bitch!"

He yanked my head back until my lips were inches from his. His body was pressed firmly against mine as he reached down to the button securing my jeans. I squirmed as hot tears spilled from my eyes. Jason grabbed my wrists, causing the zip-ties to bite against my skin, and pinned them above my head. His other hand returned to the button that was about to fail at protecting me from the guy I once loved with every part of me.

His hand wrapped tightly around my throat, immediately ceasing my screams. I struggled against his grasp and winced as he pulled down my pants and stole yet another piece of me that I would never be able to get back. I could feel myself getting light-headed as his hand remained on my throat and my spine dug into the hood of the car with each painful thrust. At that moment, as darkness settled around us and the wind whistled through the leaves on the trees, I closed my eyes and welcomed the calming effect of oblivion that was spreading through my body.

His hand slapped hard against my face, bringing me back to reality as he pulled out of me and hiked up his pants. Jason removed a pack of cigarettes from his pocket and lit one, inhaling deeply before blowing the smoke into my face.

"Thanks for that, babe. I've been so on edge, you have no idea."

Jason stumbled away, the whiskey messing with his balance as he kicked at the loose gravel and howled into the night sky, causing his cigarette to fall from his lips onto the grass. He cursed as he bent to pick it up and laughed when he fell to the ground.

I looked down at my wrists, swollen and red with dried blood, and then looked back at Jason; he was still laughing at nothing on the grass. I bit my lip and then took off towards the trees before I let hesitation get in the way. My legs propelled me forward faster than they ever had before as my lungs greedily inhaled the damp night air. It was hard to see in the thick of the forest, but I didn't let that stop me.

Branches scraped against my cheeks and hidden tree roots threatened to send me careening to the ground at any misstep. I didn't dare look behind me, but I knew he was following, his voice echoed around me, causing my skin to prickle with fear.

"You can run, but you can't hide."

Jason's taunting voice carried me through the burning fire in my lungs. This was my only chance at escape. If he caught me now, he would never let his guard down again. I slowed my pace as the trees cleared and gave way to a dirt road with old streetlights illuminating a single, faded sign. My eyes squinted as I read the worn print informing me that a rest stop was only one kilometer away. I looked into the darkness of the trees behind me. Jason's voice sounded only a short distance away. I took a deep breath and began to run, hoping that my legs would carry me the distance needed to hopefully get to safety.

A run-down building appeared in the distance. It boasted faded red shingles and brown siding accompanied by an old gas pump and a creaky porch swing that groaned with each passing breeze. The lights were off and a closed sign hung in the window. My heart filled with hope when I noticed a pay phone off to the far side of the building. I pushed myself to the limit as I hurtled towards it, my body crashing into the clear swinging doors. I grabbed the phone from the receiver and cried tears of joy when a dial tone sounded in my ear. Clumsily I held the phone to my ear, my wrists still bound with the zip-ties. My fingers shook as they dialed *9-1-1.*

"9-1-1, what's your emergency?"

"Help, please. I've been kidnapped. My name is Amy Andrews. I've been taken by my ex-boyfriend Jason Reeves. Please help me, I don't know where I am. I'm so scared!"

"Okay, Amy, try not to panic. I'm dispatching the police and we are tracing this call as we speak. Are you at a pay phone?"

"Yes, please hurry before he finds me …"

"Okay, sweetheart, just breathe. Are there any signs around you to tell you where you are?"

"No, nothing." My eyes frantically scanned the area. Everything was cast in shadows of darkness. "Oh god, it's too dark to tell! Please hurry!" I pleaded.

"We are working as quickly as we can for you, Amy. Are you hurt?"

The hairs on the back of my neck rose as a twig snapped behind me. I peered into the darkness, the phone still pressed against my ear. I listened, the silence was suffocating.

Another twig snapped, its sound echoing off the walls of the pay phone cubicle.

"I think he's here … I think he found–"

My body slumped to the ground. Blood seeped from my temple as Jason stood over me, a crowbar in hand and a face of pure and volatile rage. I struggled to stay conscious, willed myself to scream, kick, fight, anything.

He picked up the receiver dangling above me and put it to his ear. "You're too late."

His voice was like ice as he dropped the phone and raised the crowbar above his head. With all of his strength, he brought it down over and over until I was bruised, broken, and unconscious. Satisfied with his work, Jason dropped the crowbar, picked up the forgotten phone, and placed it gently back on its hook.

CHAPTER TWENTY

DETECTIVE THOMPSON

 "We traced the call," Detective Thompson told them as he answered a call on his cell phone. Amy's parents stared at him with an urgency that made him think of his own daughters at home and the unimaginable grief that losing them would bring.

 "Yes, I want the recording of the 9-1-1 call. No, we don't have time for that. Get it to me now." He shoved his phone into the small pocket of his suit and apologized for the interruption.

 "Where is she?" Amy's dad spoke first, a hint of hope lacing his words. He held his wife close as he waited anxiously.

 "The call came from an old gas station rest stop just south of here. We have the K-9 unit dispatched out there, and I will be heading there as well."

"Was she … okay?" Amy's mother's voice was barely a whisper, Detective Thompson found himself leaning closer to hear. He hesitated before answering, careful to choose his words wisely.

"We were told by the 9-1-1 operator that Amy stated Jason had taken her and she didn't know where she was. She was afraid he would find her before help arrived. The operator had said that the last thing Amy said was that Jason had found her and then all that was heard were screams. Jason came onto the phone once the screaming stopped and said, 'You're too late' before the line went dead."

Amy's parents looked away, her father's face was full of agony and rage, and her mother was sobbing loudly against his chest and praying to God to keep her baby safe.

"Do you think she's still alive? She can't be dead, for God's sake, she's only eighteen years old!" Amy's father paced the kitchen floor, his hands disheveling his hair as he lost himself in horrific thoughts of his daughter's fate.

"I apologize, but I have to leave and meet the rest of the team where the call from Amy was made."

"Can we come, too?"

"I'm sorry, Mr. Andrews, for your safety and as to not jeopardize the investigation, I have to insist that you stay here. I will keep you informed with every update, you have my word." Detective Thompson excused himself and headed towards his police cruiser. He backed out of the driveway and looked in his rearview mirror to see Amy's parents staring after him with no doubt a pit of complete dread weighing them down.

The old rest stop was crowded with police officers, SWAT, and the K-9 unit. Police tape bordered off a large area around the pay phone. Detective Thompson's stomach tightened, fearful he was late on receiving an update about a dead body, possibly Amy's. He pushed through the crowd and stepped under the police-line tape. Blood soaked the dirt-covered ground and was splattered inside the phone booth walls. He returned his gaze to the blood-soaked dirt. A trail carried on a few feet away as if the person were dragged before coming to a sudden stop next to two tire treads leading away from the scene and a bloody crowbar abandoned beside them.

Detective Thompson released the breath he'd been holding and nodded at the sheriff heading his way.

"A bloody mess, this whole thing is. The blood, the crowbar ... I will be surprised if she's still–"

"We can't draw assumptions like that. We don't know the whole story of what happened. For all we know this could be Jason's blood ..." Detective Thompson cut the sheriff off, refusing to believe for even a second that Amy Andrews was dead.

"Maybe, but Detective, the recording at the end ... Jason's words about it being too late."

"Enough, Andy. I don't want to hear it. Let's just see if the dogs have picked up a scent or any leads, and let's find her before it really is too late."

CHAPTER TWENTY-ONE

Every inch of my body radiated with a pain unlike any I had ever experienced. I tried to turn my head and cried out as splinters of fire erupted at the base of my skull. Slowly, I opened my eyes and darkness pressed against me from every angle. The hum of a moving vehicle told me I was once again in Jason's trunk. My breathing was shallow, every breath a struggle against the pain in my ribs. My head was spinning and a dense fog threatened to take away my already slipping consciousness.

I wanted to cry, yet no tears seemed to come. I had lost any remaining hope of escape. I knew that I was most likely going to die, it was just a matter of when and how. I thought about how worried Mom and Dad must be, and immediately felt guilty for lying to them.

How could I have been so stupid? So reckless and selfish? All these people had tried to keep me safe, and I went behind their backs for a love that was anything but right. I gave up everything for a complete monster, and now I was going to die at eighteen years old. The reality of everything was suffocating, and my body shook with silent cries of despair.

"Wake up!" Jason's voice was startling as my eyes flew open and took in the open trunk and Jason standing over me. He took in my sight and for a moment, a look of shame and guilt flashed across his face.

"Can you move?" His voice was gentler this time. I tried to bring my legs up and push up off the trunk with my arms, but my body trembled and collapsed with weakness.

"That's okay, I'll carry you."

He reached down and tucked one arm under my shoulders and one under my knees and lifted me out of the trunk. Sunlight burned my eyes as I closed them, my head falling against his chest. I was grateful that, for the moment, Jason was being kind and gentle. I knew if I wanted any hope in surviving this that I had to do things differently. It was time to play Jason's game.

What looked like an old abandoned farmhouse stood before us. There weren't any houses or traffic for miles. He carried me to the front door and budged it open with a shove of his shoulder. The door swung open with a loud creak and dust filled the air. We entered a narrow hallway. Jason ducked as he carried me through an arched doorway into a small living room with a fireplace. Gently, he placed me onto a worn couch and slid his rolled-up sweater under my head. I forced him a weak smile and whispered *'thank you.'*

"I'm going to go find some wood to make a fire. I won't be long." He was staring at me, as if deciding if I could be trusted or not, then remembered how I could hardly move and decided he was safe to venture off for a few minutes. I nodded in response and closed my eyes, the scent of Jason on his sweater reminding me of all the painful memories we have shared up until this point.

I must have drifted off because when I opened my eyes the room was dark, the only light coming from a burning fire. I turned my head and looked around. Jason was sitting in the chair beside the fire, staring at me.

"How are you feeling?" He stood up and crossed the room to sit beside me on the couch. My eyes met his and I tried clearing my throat to speak.

"I'm really sore ... every part of my body

hurts. I'm thirsty, I'm hungry, and I'm scared."

"I'm truly sorry things escalated the way they did. I don't enjoy hurting you, and I know things got out of hand this last time. I was so angry I couldn't see straight."

His head was in his hands as he spoke. I watched him carefully, studying his features as I planned how to respond in the most favorable way to my own well-being. *Play his game, Amy*, I told myself.

I reached my hand out until I could touch his arm. He looked at me with surprise and then relief as his hand rested on top of mine.

"Do you forgive me, babe? I'm so sorry…"

"Yes," I lied, forcing a smile as I looked into his eyes. I was surprised to see tears fall as he lay his head on my chest and hugged me tight. I winced against the pain in my ribs as my hand automatically stroked his hair with false affection.

"I do love you, you know?"

"Do you?" I replied numbly, challenging his words against my countless bruises.

"Yes, of course … I am sorry. The thought of not being with you, not being together … I can't handle it. Nothing will ever come between us. I won't allow it. It's you and me forever, babe." He lay down beside me, his face inches from mine on the large couch. Slowly, he stroked my cheek, waiting for my reply. I swallowed the lump in my throat before answering.

"You and me forever," I said with a weak smile.

Jason smiled before pressing his lips to mine, his tongue meeting mine with renewed frenzy. The taste of whiskey on his breath mixed with the metallic taste of blood from my lips. It took every bit of self-control to not turn away and be sick.

"Promise you won't try to leave me again?" Jason's voice turned serious now.

"I promise." My voice shook slightly with each word. His thumb brushed against my lips before taking hold of my chin until I was forced to make eye contact.

"Good, because if it happens again, I will kill you."

CHAPTER TWENTY-TWO

DETECTIVE THOMPSON

"What do you mean the trail is lost?!" Detective Thompson yelled into his cell phone as he paced outside the undercover cruiser. "I refuse to accept that. No. Jerrod, just shut up, please. Get your heads out of your asses and find that trail again. The K-9 should be all over this! The blood, the tire tracks, the crowbar, I mean, come on!" He opened his door, climbed in and slammed it shut, pulling on his seatbelt. He put the keys in the ignition and held the phone to his ear with his right shoulder.

"Listen," Detective Thompson began, "we're not going to stop searching. I don't care if it takes all day and all night. Amy Andrews is an eighteen-year-old woman who is scared and hurt beyond her own comprehension right now. I refuse to give up the search. I'm going to find that son-of-a-bitch Jason and have a few words with him before I ruin the rest of his measly life. Amy will be found if it's the last thing I do as detective." He clicked end on the call and tossed the phone onto the passenger seat. Taking a few steadying breaths, he put the car into drive and continued down the dirt road with his eyes on high alert.

Frustration coursed through his veins as he travelled down endless country roads, each one more deserted and unremarkable than the last. His fist angrily hit the steering wheel as he cursed under his breath. Amy's parents' faces played over and over in his mind before switching to the innocent one of Amy's the day they spoke on her front porch. If she had only listened, she'd be safe at home, not fighting for her life with her crazed ex-boyfriend. It was going to take a lot of willpower to not kill Jason when he finally found him.

It was discouraging to witness the police force already giving up on the search for Amy. Most assumed she was already dead, her body abandoned, never to be found. Detective Thompson truly felt like he was in this alone, his determination to find Amy alive never wavering. There was no way he was going to give up on her. She needed someone in her corner.

Time passed with every fleeting second more painful than the last. He wished he could freeze it, give himself a head start on Jason. He wasn't stupid. Jason was very good at going into hiding with Amy. He was careful to keep what he thought was his away from any prying eyes, making Detective Thompson's job exceptionally difficult.

The radio crackled as another officer's voice came through. "This is 401 to 382, do you copy?"
Detective Thompson picked up the two-way radio and pressed the button.

"382 to 401, what's up?" His heart was racing as he waited for a reply.

"We are on McConnor Drive, old side street just north from the gas station about an hour. We're parked down the road a bit, but the only house in sight has a red Sunfire parked out front."

Detective Thompson was already punching the street into his GPS and making a U-turn.

"What are you waiting for?! Get some back up and get in there! I'm about thirty minutes away, and we can't waste any more time."

"All right, we will update once an arrest has been made."

The radio went silent and Detective

Thompson put the pedal to the floor, the engine roaring with increasing speed. He flicked on the lights and sirens and flew down the back roads with renewed hope.

CHAPTER TWENTY-THREE

The skies were grey, the sun hidden
behind dark clouds that threatened a storm at
any moment. I was sitting on the couch, a
blanket wrapped around my knees while Jason
put more wood onto the fire. Playing his game
had been working well in my favor. He had
been kind and gentle, believing that I was once
again in love with him and his forever.

"That should warm the place up," he said,
smiling as he turned to sit beside me. I smiled
at him and gave him a quick kiss on the lips.
His hand moved to the back of my neck when I
began to pull away, and kept me in place. His
lips were firm on mine, his tongue exploring my
mouth as his hands slid under my shirt. I
closed my eyes and willed myself to play along
and get through this. His hands found my
breasts and began to explore as his lips moved

to my neck.

With one swift movement, he pulled my white t-shirt off and tossed it onto the floor. He pushed me back against the couch, his body pressing against mine. He nibbled my ear and whispered about how he missed claiming me. I couldn't help the shiver that went through my body. Jason must have mistaken it for pleasure. He undid the button on my jeans and slid them off onto the floor beside my shirt, followed by my underwear and bra. My heart was racing. I didn't want this.

Jason quickly pulled down his own jeans, not bothering to completely remove them. He seemed out of control, needing desperately to be inside me. I braced myself, taking a deep breath as he spread my trembling legs and roughly pushed inside me. I cried out in pain, my hands pushing at Jason's chest in urgency to slow down. He grabbed my wrists and pinned them above my head.

"Stay still, I really need this, babe," he said as he slammed himself into me over and over. Tears soaked my cheeks as his fingers dug into my pinned wrists. I could feel him finish, but he didn't stop. He continued to thrust again, over and over until he was shuddering with a second climax. Finally he let go of my wrists and collapsed on top of me. I cringed as he lay there, still deep inside me and making no effort to pull out.

"That was amazing. We definitely need to do that more often. It's great for my stress levels." His speech was slurred as he sloppily kissed my lips and each of my breasts, his tongue swirling around each nipple. I squirmed and tried to playfully push him away.

"You don't like me touching you?" he said, his voice serious as he looked up at me.

I began to panic as I struggled to find an excuse for my behavior. "Of course I like it, Jason. I'm just tired and cold, that's all." I kissed his lips slowly and passionately in an effort to hide my displeasure. When I pulled away he was smiling at me.

"Good, because I love your body." He pulled out of me and I winced in pain. I reached down for my clothes, but he stopped me by grabbing my hand. "Only your bra and panties."

I stared at him before nodding obediently. He told me to stand up and turn around. I felt awkward standing in the middle of the living room completely naked. Jason picked up my bra. Carefully, he slipped it on me and fastened the back before reaching down for my underwear. He came around to my front and slipped them over each foot before sliding them up my legs and backing up. He looked me up and down and smiled in approval.

"Stay like that unless I tell you otherwise, understood?" His voice was firm as he looked into my eyes.

"Okay," I whispered, and moved back to the couch and wrapped the blanket around my body.

Jason walked over to the large bay window and pulled back the yellowed curtain. Quickly, he dropped it and backed up.

"Shit! Get up, Amy."

I stood in a rush, the blanket falling to the ground. I wrapped my arms across my chest as Jason paced the living room.

"What's going on? What did you see?" I made a move towards the window to see what had caused Jason to panic. His hand gripped my upper arm and forced me away from the window until I was standing in front of him.

"I want you to hide in the pantry and not make a sound until I come and get you. Do you understand?" Jason pulled me towards the kitchen pantry as he spoke. I tried to resist and argue about what I was supposed to be hiding from.

"I'm not fucking around. Get in the damn pantry and keep your mouth shut!"

The door slammed behind me as darkness filled the small space. I felt around for a light switch without any luck. I put my ear to the door and steadied my breathing as I listened for any voices that weren't Jason's, knowing this could be my only chance at rescue.

Minutes seemed to pass agonizingly slow with no sounds of life beyond the door. I chewed my lower lip as I contemplated disobeying Jason and leaving my hiding spot. *Screw it,* I decided as I turned the handle and edged the door open. I peered around the corner to the front door; it was open but the house was silent. I pressed against the wall and crept towards the front door.

"Hold it right there! Don't move!" I jumped, startled as a police officer stood mid-way up the stairs with his gun pointed at me. I put my hands in the air as my heart hammered in my chest.

"Please, sir, I need your help."

The officer lowered his gun as he descended the stairs.

"What's your name, miss? Are you alone?"

"I'm Amy Andrews, and no, I am not alone. I've been taken by my ex-boyfriend Jason Reeves." The officer reached for his radio and held it to his lips.

"This is Officer Morrow, Amy Andrews has been found alive."

I could feel tears on my cheeks as hope

flooded my body. I was saved. I was going to be okay. ...

"Where's your back up, Officer?" Jason's cold voice echoed down the stairs into the empty doorway. Jason's hands were around Officer Morrow's neck before he had a chance to raise his gun. A sickening snap was heard as Jason released the officer's lifeless body and watched as it thudded heavily down the wooden stairs, landing by my bare feet. Blood pooled from his skull and travelled along the cold tile floor, filling in each groove as if painting a picture of my failed escape. A scream caught in my throat as my hands covered my mouth in horror. All I could do was stare at his lifeless body, my eyes wide in shock.

Jason stood on the stairs, staring at me. My eyes travelled across the floor to Officer Morrow's discarded gun. I looked back at Jason, his face knowing exactly what I was thinking.

"Don't even think about it, Amy. You touch that gun and you won't live to see another day."

"I'd rather die than spend another second with you!" I screamed. I dived across the floor, my knees landing in the pool of blood as my fingers closed around the cold steel of the gun.

I rolled onto my back, gun pointing at Jason as he walked towards me.

"You don't have the guts," he said, a sick smile playing on his lips.

My finger found the curve of the trigger as my chest heaved with adrenaline. He was looking at me like I was a sad, lost puppy and I could feel my blood boil with everything he had done to me.

"Watch me," I answered, and aimed the gun at the very thing that had countlessly taken away the part of me I could never get back. My hand was steadier than it had been in days as I pulled the trigger. My eyes closed against the sound of the bullet leaving the gun and entering Jason. I opened my eyes to see him on the floor, screaming in agony as he gripped his leg. The bullet had entered his upper leg, right beside his groin. Blood soaked his jeans and the floor, mixing with Officer Morrow's.

I stood up and stared at Jason as a sense of calm came over me. For the first time, I smiled at him and his pathetic state.

"It's kind of like poetic justice, don't you think?" I said as I made my way to the front door.

"Where do you think you're going?" Jason yelled through gritted teeth.

"Wherever the hell I want to," I said,

slamming the front door behind me.

CHAPTER TWENTY-FOUR

The evening breeze was warm against my skin. The sun was descending with an orange glow behind the fields of overgrown grass, and crickets began to sing their evening lullabies. I smiled freely for the first time in a long time as the door closed behind me. I looked around for the police car Officer Morrow would have been in, but the grass was too overgrown to see from the house. My hands rested against my bare stomach, remembering that all I had on was a bra and underwear. I glanced back at the door debating going back in for my clothes, but Jason's face and his hands violating my body flashed through my mind and caused goosebumps to erupt across my skin. I shook my head and made my first step to freedom as my bare feet crunched down on the gravel drive.

The road was long and empty as I made my way in no particular direction. All I knew was that I wanted to get as far away from Jason and that house as I possibly could. Officer Morrow's police car came into view after a few minutes of walking. I found myself running towards it, praying desperately that the keys were still inside. My fingers closed around the cool handle of the door and a breath of relief came as it opened with a small creak. I slid into the seat and looked at the ignition: no keys. *Shit.* My brain went into overdrive as I battled the possibility of having to go back into that house. I looked at the passenger seat but only saw a pack of cigarettes. I reached for the glove box and frowned when that too came up empty. Slowly, I opened the center console between the driver and passenger seats and felt tears prick my eyes as the keys to my freedom appeared.

I put them into the ignition and turned. The engine roared to life as my heart raced with anticipation. *This is it, Amy. The moment you've been waiting for. Now, drive!*

I pulled the car into drive and headed down the winding road, my prison and my hell fading in the rearview mirror. I couldn't wait to see Mom and Dad. I imagined pulling into the driveway and the look on their faces when I got out. I missed them so much. And Trish … God how I missed my best friend.

I turned the heat on as the setting sun disappeared and twilight took its place. I chanced a glance in the rearview mirror at myself and cringed; I looked awful. Purple-and-black bruises marked my face, but my green eyes still held a sparkle of fight in them. *I have won,* I told myself over and over as the roads stretched ahead of me.

A gas station came into view hours later. I held my stomach as it growled painfully with hunger. I didn't dare stop though. I was terrified that if I stopped for even just a minute that Jason would find me and it would be game over. I had come too far to lose to an empty stomach.

An hour and a half later, distant lights of a town came into view. I accelerated as hope burned through my veins and the taste of freedom filled my senses. A sign for my home town flew by as I continued to speed down the road until civilization and familiarity surrounded me. It was like a warm hug after doing the polar dip in the middle of winter. I thought about going straight to the police station, but my heart had other plans as I turned down my own street and felt hot tears slide down my cheeks as my home came into view.

I pulled into the driveway and swung open the door. The front porch lights flicked on as my dad appeared in the doorway.

"Amy! Oh my God, you're okay!" He was running across the grass, my own legs propelling me into his arms where I collapsed in a pile of exhaustion and safety. He picked me up and carried me towards the front door as Mom came out in her night robe. Her hand was over her mouth in shock, and tears streamed down her face. She stroked my hair as Dad carried me into the house and placed me on the couch. Mom brought over a fleece blanket and wrapped it around my exposed body. The shivers I didn't realize I had subsided as exhaustion made way to sleep and I drifted off with no fear of what might happen to me when I closed my eyes.

∞ ∞ ∞

"We have to call the police," Mrs. Andrews said. "Do you have Detective Thompson's card still?"

"Of course I do, hang on." He grabbed the cordless phone and dialed. "Detective Thompson, you're not going to believe this. Amy's home. She showed up in a police cruiser. She's asleep right now. No, there wasn't an officer with her, she was driving.

Okay, see you shortly." He clicked end on the phone and sat down, his hand protectively resting on his daughter's leg.

"What did he say?" Mom asked.

"He's going to check the house where the officer of this car was sent to and see what happened, and then he is coming here." Dad rubbed his face, bags hung below his eyes in dark circles.

"You should sleep, dear," she said softly, stroking her husband's cheek.

"No," he replied firmly. "No way in hell am I leaving her side for a second."

CHAPTER TWENTY-FIVE

DETECTIVE THOMPSON

The sky was dark by the time he arrived at the old house. Shadows fell across the ground in odd shapes and the air remained unusually still. Detective Thompson turned off the ignition and stepped out onto the gravel drive. Jason's red Sunfire remained parked next to the house.

He made his way towards the front door, his gun aimed and ready. The house was dark, the windows void of any light. Something wasn't right. Officer Morrow had stopped responding to his radio, Amy had escaped with his police cruiser, and Jason was possibly just ten feet away from him at this very moment.

The handle on the door was cool against his hand as he turned it slowly. With a creak, he opened it only a fraction before stepping back. Pulling his flashlight from his duty belt, Detective Thompson secured it against the steel of his gun. Swiftly, his boot slammed against the door, sending it colliding into the wall behind it with a deafening crash.

"This is the police. Drop your weapons and put your hands up!" His voice echoed against the barren walls. He darted his flashlight from the empty staircase down to the lifeless body of Officer Morrow just inches away.

"Shit!" Detective Thompson lowered his gun and knelt beside his fellow colleague, his fingers pressed against the officer's neck. He already knew he was dead but needed the confirmation.

Not far from the officer's body, a trail of blood travelled from the bottom of the stairs and down the hallway. It was thin and looked as if a body had been dragged, leaving a path of sustained injury behind. He stepped over Officer Morrow's body and aimed his light on the blood trail, his pulse quickening and sweat forming on his brows with each echo of his footsteps.

"Jason Reeves, this is Detective Thompson. If you are in this house, I demand you answer me and relinquish any weapons."

Silence, followed by the slamming of a

door, led Detective Thompson down the hall to the living room. Someone was here. Blood soaked the carpet and trailed in tiny drops through the kitchen, stopping at the basement door. He cursed under his breath when the door didn't budge, locked from the inside as if mocking him.

His boot slammed into the door, rattling it on its hinges. The lock held strong. Stepping back, Detective Thompson lunged at the door, his shoulder crashing into it with all his weight. The lock released against the blow, causing the door to swing open on two remaining hinges. Wasting no time, he made his way down the stairs with his gun at the ready.

The baseball bat collided with Detective Thompson's ribs right as he reached the bottom of the stairs, sending his gun and flashlight sliding across the cement floor. Jason was relentless, swinging the bat over and over, trying to make contact in the dark space. He grabbed Jason's wrist, stopping him mid-swing and twisted it around his back.

"Drop the weapon, Jason! Now!"

Jason continued to struggle against Detective Thompson's grip. He twisted harder before dropping to his knees with a loud cry.

"You're fucking hurting me!"

Detective Thompson reached for his

handcuffs. Jason took this opportunity to swing his free arm backwards, his nails making contact with his eyes. In a moment of blindness, Detective Thompson's grip loosened and Jason bound to his feet. Picking up the baseball bat, he brought it down on his leg. Detective Thompson cried out in pain as a sickening crack made Jason smile.

"Good luck catching me now, Detective. I think I will go retrieve my girlfriend." He dropped the bat and made his way up the stairs.

"You get back here! You're not going to get away with this. Everyone is looking for you!" Jason laughed in response to his threats. Detective Thompson cursed loudly. How could he have let his guard down? He reached for his radio and switched it on.

"This is Detective Thompson, I need back up. Jason has escaped. He will be driving a red Sunfire, possibly even my undercover cruiser. He is most likely armed and dangerous. Officer Morrow has been killed, and Jason is heading for Amy. Protect her, and send me an ambulance." He dropped the radio; it hung against his chest as he steadied his breathing through the eruption of pain in his left leg.

∞ ∞ ∞

Jason

Jason climbed into the undercover cruiser. The keys dangled in the ignition, inviting his escape. He would be less conspicuous than in his red car. The engine roared to life as he backed out of the drive and headed down the road, leaving Detective Thompson and his hateful words behind. He wasn't a monster, he did love Amy, and she loved him. Everything he did to her he did out of love. Why couldn't anybody see this?

Almost two hours passed when his hometown came into view. He could feel excitement build at the thought of holding Amy in his arms again. He would forgive her for leaving, but would have to punish her for being so careless. She needed to know her place, and that place was with him. It only took minutes to get to Amy's street, memories played as he pulled into her drive and got out of the car. The front door swung open as Amy's dad ran out with his cell phone pressed to his ear; no doubt calling the police.

"What the hell do you think you're doing showing up here!?"

"I've come for my girlfriend. Is she inside?"

"You're not going anywhere near my daughter. I've called the police and they're on their way."

Jason could see the fear in his face, the

pulse in his neck bounding with panic as he tried to protect his little girl. He smiled before pulling the gun from his waistband and pointing it at Amy's father.

"I suggest you move." Jason said coldly.

"No."

"What's going on? Who's at the door?" Mrs. Andrews came to the door, her hand quickly coming to her lips.

"Go to Amy, now. Go somewhere safe!" he warned his wife. Jason laughed before returning his gaze to Mr. Andrews.

"I'm going to ask you one more time to move." Mr. Andrews shook his head, ignoring the gun pointed in his face.

Jason admired his courage to protect Amy, but it was no match to overpower the love he had for her. They were going to spend eternity together, even if forever meant six feet under.

Sirens echoed in the distance; they were close and time was running out.

"Move!" Jason spat, his patience wavering.

"Not a chance. You'll have to kill me first." Mr. Andrews stood firmly at the door.

Jason pulled the trigger without a second thought. The bullet entered Mr. Andrews' chest as blood splattered the door frame. He could hear his wife screaming as she watched in horror as her husband collapsed to the ground.

"Please don't hurt her. Leave us be!" She was pleading, holding Amy tight in her arms.

Jason looked into Amy's eyes. She was staring at him, tears soaking her cheeks.

"Please, Jason, if you love me, let me go."

He had missed the sound of her voice. He did love her, but there was no way he could let her go. Life wasn't worth living if she wasn't in it.

"I can't. We belong together."

"No, we don't. This isn't love, Jason." She pulled out of her mother's arms and stepped towards him. "Do the right thing while you can. Put the gun down, please."

Jason studied her face, the soft pale skin, the freckles on her nose, and the pale pink of her lips. He reached out and touched her cheek. "I love you."

Amy closed her eyes at his words and shook her head. He felt a stab of betrayal as she stepped away from him. He could hear tires screech as multiple police surrounded the property. Jason grabbed Amy by the hair and pulled her against him, her back against his chest and the gun resting against her temple.

"Jason, please don't!" She was crying, her tears soaking the arm he had around her neck.

"We belong together," Jason said as he walked her out the front door and onto the grass. Guns were pointed at him from every angle. He knew he wasn't going to make it out of here alive. This was her fault. Had she not tried to leave him, they would be safe and sound.

"Don't do it," an officer's voice sounded over a megaphone. "Let her go, Jason."

Jason shook his head, and pressed the gun deeper into Amy's temple.

∞ ∞ ∞

Amy

I winced in pain and closed my eyes, bracing for the impact of a bullet entering my skull. I heard the shot and waited, expecting to feel the sickening warmth of my blood cascading down my face. Instead, I felt Jason's body topple heavily to the ground, bringing me down with him. An officer was pulling me to my feet and carrying me away before I could make sense of what had happened. I tried to look back but my vision was blurring. The only images burned into my mind were the lifeless bodies of my father and Jason before reality slipped away.

CHAPTER TWENTY-SIX

It was two weeks before Dad was released from the hospital, and on more than one occasion it was touch-and-go on whether he was going to pull through or not. The bullet had entered his chest and caused mass amounts of internal bleeding; he was fortunate to be alive. The nurse wheeled him to the car and I helped him into the front seat and thanked her for everything she and the doctors had done.

I had only spent three days in hospital, my main injuries being cracked ribs and a ton of psychological trauma. I couldn't even count on both hands how many counsellors and sexual assault crisis workers I spoke to in those three days. It was a comforting feeling when the three of us arrived home and walked through the front door. We were alive, we were safe, and most importantly, we were together again.

I sat on the couch next to Dad while Mom made dinner in the kitchen. He leaned over and kissed the top of my head, a simple gesture that spoke endless words of love. I smiled at him and put Survivor on the TV; our favorite show. I opened my phone to three missed texts from Trish.

> *Trish: I miss you girl, so glad you're home safe and sound. I can't help but feel this is all my fault!*
> *Amy: I miss you too! Not your fault, please don't think that; you were only doing what I asked you to. Want to hang out tomorrow?*
> *Trish: Yes! Can't wait <3*

Jason had been treated at the hospital for his gunshot wound and then placed into custody. He was facing numerous charges including assault with a deadly weapon, aggravated assault, sexual assault, kidnapping, and murder in the first degree. Jason was sentenced to twenty-five years in a federal penitentiary with a chance of parole after fifteen years.

This should have been comforting as I watched from the wooden bench as the judge dismissed the court; however, my stomach knotted as Jason was hauled off with police escort, his ankles and wrists cuffed. He looked back at me and smiled with a gleam in his eye, a look that made my skin crawl and my throat go dry. I looked down at my lap until the door closed behind him and people began to leave.

Mom and Dad took my hand and helped me to my feet. We silently exited the court room and met with Detective Thompson around the corner.

"You doing okay, kid?" He smiled as he squeezed my shoulder. I nodded, suddenly finding it hard to speak.

"I know that wasn't easy to watch in there and to hear. Jason is going away for a very, very long time now, and you can move towards healing. Any college plans?" He was trying to change the subject and ease my mind, and I appreciated his efforts.

"Nothing definitive yet, still deciding what I want to do with my life."

"Maybe something in the criminal justice system?" Detective Thompson said with a wink.

"Who knows what the future holds," I replied, giving him a small smile.

"I have a meeting to attend, but please don't hesitate to contact me with anything, okay?"

I nodded and thanked him for everything.

He hugged me tightly and slipped another one of his cards into my hand before hurrying off down the hallway. I don't think I would ever be able to thank him enough for all that he had done.

The night was full of restless sleep and haunting dreams. I tossed and turned, trapped in my own hell and dark memories. I was grateful when the sun began to shine through my windows and I could leave the recluse of my room. It was no longer comforting to be there. It felt empty, haunting, and lonely. The morning passed quickly, busy with chatter and Saturday morning TV. Trish showed up at twelve thirty and we headed off in her car to grab some lunch.

"How are you doing, hun? You look fantastic!"

"I'm okay. I slept like crap last night, kept having nightmares about everything. The counsellor says this is normal and is a part of the healing process."

"I can't even imagine what kind of hellish dreams you'd be experiencing after the nightmare you've been through. When do you see the counsellor again?"

"Tuesday afternoon. She's really nice. I just can't help but feel awkward sitting in this fancy office and talking to a complete stranger about everything I've been through."

"You know I'm always here too if you ever want to talk to someone you know. I love you, Amy, and you scared the shit out of me. I thought I was never going to see you again." Trish wiped a tear from her eye and cursed under her breath. I laughed and lightly squeezed her hand.

"We're best friends, basically sisters. Face it, girl, you're stuck with me!"

"Good! Now let's get out of this car and go eat some pizza!"

We were halfway through our pepperoni pizza when the nausea set in. I clutched my stomach and paused with the slice halfway to my mouth.

"What's wrong?" Trish asked.

"I don't feel so good. I think I might be sick." I stood up and hurried towards the bathroom. I could feel my mouth water and my stomach churn as it prepped to empty its contents. I leaned over the toilet and heaved, coughing as my eyes watered. I hated being sick. It had been years, and I definitely didn't miss it. *What the hell?* I thought to myself as I washed my face and hands and made my way back to our table.

"You okay? You look pretty pale."

"Yeah," I said, as I took a sip of my water.

"I think I just ate too much maybe ..."

Trish signaled for the waitress and asked for a to-go container to pack up the rest of the pizza. We headed back towards my place in a comfortable silence, listening to the radio playing country tunes.

"Do you want this for later?" Trish asked as we pulled into my driveway. I shook my head.

"No way. One time being sick is enough to last me the next few months." She laughed and threw the box into the back seat before coming around the car and wrapping her arms around me for a tight hug.

"I love you. Text me anytime, day or night. I'm always here for you, and anytime you need some company I'm only a phone call away, okay?"

"I know. Thanks for lunch today, Trish. I love you, too. Drive safe and text me when you're home."

"Will do! Feel better, babe!" I waved as she drove off and I made my way into the house.

"How was lunch?" Mom asked. She was sitting beside Dad, watching a sitcom on TV. I sat down beside her and leaned my head on her shoulder. I suddenly felt exhausted.

"You feeling okay, hun?"

"I think I ate too much or something. I was sick at lunch, and I'm feeling pretty tired."

"Did you sleep okay?"

I shook my head.

"Have you been taking the sleeping pills the doctor prescribed you?"

"No, they make me nervous."

"Amy, you need to take these things so you can get the rest you need."

"I know. I will tonight, I promise."

I kept my promise and took my sleeping pill. It worked quickly, dissolving under my tongue and making the world slowly float away. I slept soundly, no dreams, no tossing and turning. I awoke the next morning feeling more refreshed, and silly for having not taken the sleeping pills the last few weeks. I made my way down the stairs to the smell of bacon frying, and Mom and Dad talking over coffee.

"Good morning, sweetie. How did you sleep?"

"Good. The pill worked well." The smell of the bacon grease jolted my stomach and I feared I was going to be sick again.

"Still feeling unwell?" Mom looked concerned as she came over and felt my forehead. "You don't feel feverish."

"I'm sure it will pass, Mom, don't worry."

My cell phone rang and I excused myself as I left the kitchen.

"Hello?" I answered.

"Good morning. This is Anderson Health Centre. May I speak with Amy Andrews, please?"

"This is she," I replied as I stepped out onto the front porch.

"Hi, Amy, this is Doctor Marshall. I am calling with some news on the bloodwork you had done."

I swallowed nervously. It was never a good thing to receive calls about blood tests.

"Is everything okay?" I asked.

"Well, as you know, we ran a full panel on your blood and I have one test result to report to you. Are you sitting down?"

"Yes," I lied, my hands starting to shake as I wracked my brain for what it could be.

"Your HCG came back elevated. You're pregnant, Amy."

My mouth dropped open as I stumbled back against the wall and slid down until I was sitting on the wooden porch. *Pregnant…* there was no way. It's not possible. Suddenly it all made sense; the nausea, the vomiting, the exhaustion … how could I not have realized? All those times he raped me with no protection, no birth control …

"Are you still there?" Her voice brought me back to reality.

"Y-yes," I stammered. "I'm still here."

"Do you have any questions?"

"No," I replied quietly.

"You will be making a follow-up appointment with your family doctor, correct?" I nodded before remembering she couldn't see me.

"Yes," I answered.

She wished me a pleasant day before hanging up, her voice cheery, not realizing the swirling horror that circled me in this never-ending nightmare.

I was pregnant, with Jason's baby...

CHAPTER TWENTY-SEVEN

Eight Months Later…

My arm rested protectively around my stomach as the car came to a stop. I unfastened my seatbelt and picked up my purse from beside my feet.

"You're sure you want to do this?" Detective Thompson was looking at me with the face of a concerned father. I gave him a small smile and nodded.

"I need to do this. It's the only way to find the closure I need."

He gave me a knowing nod and made his way around the car to my door. Detective Thompson helped me to my feet before closing the door behind me. The damp May wind threatened my exposed skin as a chill ran bone-deep. I looked down at my stomach, now so round I could no longer see my toes. I looked up at the federal prison and felt a shudder travel down my spine. It was dull and ominous-looking with its grey brick exterior and stationed guards at multiple posts around the facility.

My heart began to race as we made our way through the security and came to the registration area.

"Who are you here to see today?"

"Jason Reeves," Detective Thompson answered for me. I smiled at him gratefully.

"Can you write your name and the time in this binder, please?" The clerk passed a binder and pen through a slot in the glass window. Detective Thompson pushed them my way to complete. I picked up the pen and began to sign my name, my hand shaking slightly as the reality of what was about to happen sunk in.

"Right this way." A tall guard with dark skin and eyes of steel walked ahead of us in brisk strides. I struggled to keep up, my once graceful legs now barely managing the dreaded pregnancy waddle as we made our way down the corridor to the Maximum Security area.

It had taken a long time to realize that coming here today was what I needed to do. The moment I had found out I was pregnant, and with Jason's baby no less, had been life-changing. Just as my hands rested on my stomach now, they had instinctively done the same thing upon first hearing I was expecting. I had anticipated rage to course through me; rage, sadness, and shame, however, all I had felt was love and an overwhelming sense of calm. My therapist had explained it to me as sensing something good and beautiful emerging out of something terrible. My parents had naturally panicked, as most people would in my particular situation, but they had supported my decision to keep the baby and vowed to help in any way they could.

The guard came to a stop as he scanned his badge and unlocked the door. We stepped through and made our way down a smaller corridor before stopping in front of a steel door with a small barred window and a guard standing beside it.

"This will be where you visit with the prisoner. You get forty-five minutes but can leave anytime by alerting the guard who will be in the room during the visitation."

He was speaking, explaining the process, but all I heard was *prisoner.* Even after eight months, it still felt strange to refer to him as such. He was Jason; he would always be Jason. The guy I had loved, and then the guy I had hated. It took me months to rid myself of his toxic poison. My mind and body had been drenched in the aftermath of what he had done to me. I came here today a new person. Stronger. Smarter. Braver. He no longer owned my body, his words no longer claimed space in my mind. I had mentally evicted him from every single part of me and it was liberating.

"Ready?" Detective Thompson asked.

"More than ever," I replied as I walked into the small, dimly lit room and took my seat at the table.

"I'll go get the prisoner," the guard we had been following said, speaking to his colleague stationed in the corner of the room. He nodded in acknowledgement and turned his attention on me with a warm smile. I returned the smile and wrapped my arms protectively under my belly. A small kick sent a fluttering sensation across my stomach and caused me to smile as I adjusted myself in my seat.

"How far along are you?" the guard asked.

"Nine months," I replied.

"Congratulations." He smiled kindly.

The door opened and Jason was escorted in. His eyes met mine and in an instant the air rushed out of my lungs, leaving me breathless. I tried to compose myself as his eyes drifted to my stomach and realization registered on his face. We sat at the table in silence for what felt like an eternity before his eyes finally found my face again.

"You're pregnant," he said, his hands resting on the table, the steel handcuffs seeming louder than normal as he fidgeted and they made contact with the table.

"Yes," I said. Proud of the strength in my voice.

"Girl or boy?"

"Girl."

Jason let out a heavy sigh and brought his hands to his face. He looked pained, sick almost, as he looked from my face to my stomach. I tried to imagine what must be going through his mind. Shock and guilt? Or maybe anger and resentment?

"What's her name?"

"Pardon?" I asked.

"What are you going to name her?" he repeated.

I thought for a moment as I looked down at my stomach and smiled.

"Grace," I answered. The name coming to me only at that very moment. I looked up at him and finally was able to see him for what he was. *Nothing.* He was nothing but a fragment of my memory. A page in the chapter of my past, a tarnished book long since forgotten.

"I've missed you." His voice broke my

thoughts and brought me back to reality.

"You've missed me?" I said, the disgust clear in my words. "Are you serious?"

"Do you miss me?" He tried reaching for my hand across the table. I pulled back quickly and pushed my chair back a few inches.

"You are a delusional idiot if you think for a second that I could possibly miss you," I spat, the words spewing from my mouth like arrows to his heart.

He looked down at his hands, still outstretched, and slowly brought them back to his lap.

"Are you going to tell her about me?" he asked. "Will Grace know that I'm her dad?"

"Would you want your daughter to know the monster her dad is?" My voice was icy as I waited for his reply.

"No," he said, to my surprise.

"Then we agree on something." I started to get up from my chair, feeling exhausted already from the short interaction.

"Wait," he said, standing from his chair.

The guard stepped forward, anticipating Jason's next move to be a foolish one.

"What is it?" I asked.

"Can I … can I feel her?" He looked into my green eyes and pleaded silently. Part of me wanted to tell him to get a life, while the other part felt compelled to fulfill his one wish with the daughter he would never be permitted to raise.

"Okay," I agreed reluctantly and stepped towards him. His hands reached out and rested on the top of my belly. Though his hands were warm, they still sent a chill down my spine.

"Hi, Grace," he began, "it's your daddy. I'm sorry we won't get to meet, but I bet you're going to be beautiful."

I felt myself fighting back tears when suddenly a hard kick nudged his hands. His smile grew wide but quickly disappeared when I stepped back.

"That was amazing," he said, his voice full of emotion. "Will you be back?" he asked as I made my way towards the door.

"No, Jason, I won't. This is it. Take a good look at everything you will be missing. When you go to sleep at night I hope you remember this. Remember the moment you felt your daughter move, and remember the moment you watched us walk away. This is your fault and your punishment. You may have poisoned my past, but you will never take my future from me."

I didn't look back to see his reaction. I didn't care. I had said what I needed to say and I walked out of that jail feeling stronger and more capable than ever before.

I wrapped my arms around my stomach and thanked Grace for giving me something to hold onto. She gave me purpose, she gave me light, and she gave me hope. Without her, I know I would have lost myself, succumbed to the bitter memories and invisible scars. It was rare to find something so beautiful nestled deep within a nightmare so dark and empty. That alone taught me a strength that only a warrior could know, and a warrior I was.

ABOUT THE AUTHOR

Heather was born and raised in Ontario, Canada. She spends her days helping others as a Registered Practical Nurse while also raising her little girl.

Writing has been a passion for Heather as long as she can remember and it is with great enthusiasm that she introduces her first novel. Based on the struggles of high school and relationships, 'The Way He Loved Me' brings the reader down a road that is all too familiar to most. The author hopes the book will help young adults to recognize the warning signs of an abusive relationship before it is too late.

No woman should endure domestic abuse. Heather wants all women to understand that they are beautiful, special and deserving of love and respect.

Made in the USA
Monee, IL
25 June 2021